BORN
TO
TRAVEL
THEWORLD

To my dear friend,
an auditor as my book,
with many thanks for a
job well done!!

Jovino A. Rodriguez

January 3, 2023

BORN

TO

TRAVEL

THE WORLD

A LITTLE BOY WITH HUMBLE BEGINNINGS MADE HIS DREAM A REALITY

LOUIS RODRIGUEZ

ISBN: 978-1-7329021-2-1 (Paperback)
ISBN: 978-1-7329021-1-4 (eBook)

Front cover and book design by Author

Second printing 2019
Publisher
Louis Rodriguez
8 Warren Drive
Marlboro NJ 07746

To my daughters, Alice and Marie, and to my sons, Louis and David, to whom I wish to express my gratitude that despite my absence they became successful professionals, are happily married and dedicated with intense feelings of love to my grandchildren; Stephen, Scott, Alexa, Nicole, Callum and Kataryna.

Contents

Part One

From Childhood to Youth

Chapter 1

My Home and City

COLOMBIA, LOCATED at the northern part of South America, is a country of luxuriant rainforest, towering mountains and coffee plantations. Bogotá, the capital, is the largest city in Colombia and one of the largest in Latin America. It is among the 30 largest cities of the world and the third-highest capital city in South America at 8,612 feet above sea level, after Quito and La Paz.

Candelaria is a historic neighborhood in high-altitude Bogotá, well known for its colonial old buildings. Its well-known attractions include Bolivar Square, Casa del Florero (Flower Vase Home), the Gold Museum and the Fernando Botero Museum, a tribute to Colombian artist Fernando Botero, South America's most famous painter, famous for his smooth, bloated shapes of people. The neighborhood also boasts the Main Cathedral, Candelaria Church, restaurants, bars, shopping and, best of all, its location near the foothills of Monserrate Mountain with an altitude of about 10,365 feet in the Andes mountain range. Candelaria's architecture in its old houses, churches and buildings has Spanish colonial, Baroque and art deco styles.

The story of my life begins in this neighborhood of Candelaria. I lived in a traditional single-story house laid around a central patio, reflecting the typical Andalucía style found in Spain as well as in colonial Candelaria. The streets are hilly and narrow with space for one car going in one direction only. In a similar manner, sidewalks within Candelaria's colonial area are also narrow with just enough space for two average-sized persons walking tightly side by side.

From south to north, Candelaria is located between 6th Street and Jimenez Avenue, and from east to west are Circunvalar to Eighth Avenues. Candelaria's central point is Bolivar Square, in memory of the liberator Simon Bolivar since 1846. It is said that the city of Bogotá began here with the erection of 12 huts. It was also here where the first stones were laid for Colombia's Main Cathedral. Bolivar Square represents an important sector of Colombia and includes other major institutions such as the Congress of the Republic, the Judicial Courts Palace, the Mayor's Office, San Bartolome College and, in one corner of the square, the July 20th House, also referred to as the Flower Vase Home (Casa del Florero) where the Shout of Independence was first given. It was here on July 20th, 1810 that the Creole (locals with Spanish ancestors) rebellion against Spanish Rule broke out. It was here where independence began and was attained nine years later. The sector also includes several universities, libraries, and museums.

I was born four blocks away from Bolivar Square, on Third Avenue between 12th and 13th Streets. The Barrio of Candelaria was partially preserved as a colonial sector of the original town. I look back and have nothing but lovely memories of my childhood. My neighborhood was not far from the most important sector of the Capital. It was, and still is, a poor neighborhood consisting of honest working-class people. The old Spanish homes had many rooms built around the large patios. These patios in general were square in shape with a drainage located in the center where rainwater was released to the sewage system. There were a few homeowners who sublet individual empty rooms. My mom always rented one of these rooms.

Tenants would share a single toilet and a single shower room, taking turns to shower with warm water. The water tank contained an electric coil as a heating device to keep the water warm. However, one had to be careful to not take long showers because it would soon turn into a cold shower. We had to make sure we took our weekly showers at times when the lines of waiting tenants were shorter.

I grew up living with my mom in a single room crowded with miscellaneous non-matching pieces of furniture. It usually included a double bed, an armoire for storing our best clothes and a footlocker. There were also one or two stools with three or four legs and no back or armrests for my mom's few, rarely visiting friends and for my grandmother or my uncle when they came to visit. The place was usually so tight that my knees and shins were always bruised from hitting various wooden pieces that filled the room. One light bulb hung in the center of the room and we had no electrical outlets to add small lamps or connect a small radio. My entire family consisted of my mom Alicia, my grandmother Mercedes and my uncle Luis Bernardo, who did not live with us but occasionally visited.

My grandmother and my mom regularly had strong arguments. I was around five years old and could not understand what they were arguing about. But I always felt sorry for my grandmother because it seemed she always lost the arguments and at times I saw her crying quietly with tears running down her fair-complexion cheeks. My grandmother was diabetic and died years later from this ugly disease. She was constantly thirsty and eagerly gulped down a few sodas during the day. If she knew then what we know now about the amount of sugar contained in a bottle of soda and the impact on her diabetic condition, she would have drunk water all the time. My grandmother must have been very pretty in her youth. She had green eyes, light sandy hair, fair complexion and was rather tall and elegant.

My uncle Luis Bernardo, who never went to college, enrolled in the Colombian Army and served for many years and rose to become a noncommissioned officer. He was always out of town in one state (known in Colombia as department) or another. At one time he was mayor of a small town in the department of Tolima. He was a beer drinker and his only form of entertainment was to get drunk as often as possible. He was also a womanizer, as reported by my grandma and my mom. Again, he would visit his mom and my mom occasionally.

These were my family. I never met my father or anybody from his family. I have vague memories of what he looked like because when I was an adult my mom showed me his picture. I must say that, in my opinion I never looked like him. He appeared to be short, perhaps 5 feet, 3 inches tall, frail looking and not handsome at all, while I grew up to be 5 feet, 11 inches. At times, I think perhaps my mom pointed at the wrong man in the group photograph or else I may have looked at the wrong person. I think I may have his brains, but since I never met him, I don't know, although I believe I have my mom's intelligence. I always considered her a smart person with a strong personality and bad temper.

My mom always meant well when she was bringing me up by herself without the support of a father. She wanted the best for me as moms usually do for their children. She barely was able to read and write. She descended from a family with a similar educational background that moved from Colombia's rural areas to the urban barrios of Bogotá. They believed that having male children was best for any family as they could grow up and get jobs at the earliest possible age to assist in sustaining the family. Educating me to the point of attending high school for a better life was never on my mom's horizon. She thought it would be unattainable because of the cost associated with tuition fees, plus the fact that no one in her family had ever completed high school. I do not blame her for the way she thought about it. Along with her low income, she obviously was brought up with the belief that she must follow family traditions and that the sooner I started working the sooner additional income would flow into the family.

My mom, despite her lack of education, was an entrepreneurial lady. She rented store space at Calle Del Embudo, one of the narrowest and prettiest streets in

Candelaria. She felt that that was an important location within the neighborhood suitable to sell milk. Within a few days, she purchased the necessary components: a table, a container sufficiently large to accommodate 30 liters of milk, and a one-liter aluminum pitcher to scoop the milk out from the large container for selling to clientele. The milk was delivered to the store in large 10-gallon (19-liter) aluminum containers early in the morning. She would sell the milk in one-liter portions to neighboring residents from early morning hours until about noon or when she ran out of milk. Then she locked the place and went home.

At the time, I had no brothers or sisters. I was lonely all the time except for my mom who was around me most of the time. In addition, I was introverted. When adults were present, and my mom was talking to them, if I happened to say something that made sense to me but not to my mom, she would scream at me, shouting that it was an adult conversation and I should stay out of it for my own good. I never had any toys to play with, so I learned to play with my hands projecting shadows on the wall or moving my fingers in such a way to amaze others. I used to play with small and empty matchstick boxes. Back then, matchsticks were packed in two-by-three-inch carton containers and sold to cigarette smokers and others. I used to make tiny little trucks to play with. Also, I learned to make miscellaneous items with sheets of newspapers: hats, airplanes and origami figures, folding the paper to make various shapes such as birds. My favorite origami was paper planes of various sizes that I made from old newspaper or notebooks sheets.

My mom was also a very religious person. Every Sunday she used to take me to the Candelaria Church for the 12-noon catholic mass, when the sun was bright and church goers wore their best clothes. Since I was an only child, I had to go with my mom wherever she went. That is where my religious beliefs come from and to this day, I rarely miss mass on Sundays. The Colombian traditional Christmas season was very nice throughout my neighborhood. There were firecrackers, miscellaneous fireworks, hand-held noise makers, balloons, "faroles" (paper lanterns with a lit candle stick located in the center of the lantern) hanging from front doors of most homes, and, of course, singing of Christmas carols and special dinners celebrating Christmas. These daily celebrations started December 16 and continued through December 24 when Jesus was born. Families that owned homes took turns having at least one party over each of the nine days leading to the 24th, when the largest celebration of all took place. My mom and I used to get up early in the morning, about 4 a.m. and walk 13 blocks to the San Francisco church where she knew they had daily mass. But this was not just your regular mass. It was a special mass where priests and deacons worked every single day to set up the altar with the nativity display beginning December 16. Nativity refers to the birth of Jesus. When Jesus' parents, Mary and Joseph, traveled from Nazareth to Bethlehem to be counted in a government census, they found that there was no room for them in the local inn. I visualized this as a nine-day soap opera, and I was eager to see the changes in the nativity display each day. Throughout the mass, Christmas carols were sung by children my age. In addition to singing, they blew water whistles simulating birds. All the children, including me, looked forward to the arrival of Jesus at midnight December 24 because it was Jesus who brought toys to us. It was the only time when I found small toys on my bed, a bed that I shared with my mom.

Twice a year, my mom used to pray the catholic novena for nine consecutive days. Christmas was one of them. That remains an unforgettable activity for me, where my mom and I spent quality time together that was repeated every year during the month of December. My mom took advantage of any catholic celebration to pray. She had nobody to look after me, no other family member or friend that she trusted, therefore wherever she had to go, I had to go along with her whether I liked it or not.

I do not remember what period of the year it was the second time she prayed the novena, but I'll never forget the creepy, weird place and eerie time. I don't believe she was an obsessed religious person who was out of control, but rather a lady of faith who strongly believed in God. She, in addition to her faith in God, also believed in the miracles made by the souls of those that departed this earth to the other world, perhaps to heaven. Consequently, whenever that time for the second novena came, she would get me ready, dress me up warmly and out we went about 9 PM to the main gates of Central Cemetery of Bogotá. We visited the cemetery every consecutive night for nine nights to pray to the Lord and to the souls for a specific purpose or need she had. We were not alone kneeling in front of the locked gates. There were others, kneeling and praying, just like my mom on the rough cement. Since I was a child of about six or seven, I was not asked to get on my knees. The first few nights when we started coming were the worst for me until I got used to the conditions. These other believers brought candles which they lit to provide some dim lighting near the gates. All these people were praying at the same time although not in unison, which created a confusing murmur that broke the silence of the eerie surroundings. I'd look through the steel gate bars very carefully, observing that all was quiet, and it seemed to me that there were many shadows moving back and forth over the tombstones. I thought that soon all the souls would be popping out of their tombs to grab me and my mom. Although I tried to believe that the souls were keeping an eye on us, it was kind of scary. I used to hold my mom's coat very tightly. It helped calm me while I waited for my mom to finish her prayers, but I was not too pleased at having to be there. As the novena days went by, I became accustomed to the nightly cemetery visits. My mother believed that this was one of the greatest acts of charity that one could perform. Our prayers would help the souls during their time in Purgatory, so that they could enter more quickly into the abundance of heaven. She would offer a novena on behalf of the dead, as designated by the church as a prayer for the faithful departed. There was nothing wrong with that, except that the convenience store was closed earlier than usual for about nine evenings.

Chapter 2

Younger Years

WHEN I REACHED the age of eight in 1946, my mom felt it was time for me to begin learning how to read. She believed that starting school before eight was too early and that I would drop out of school too soon. She found a small private school not too far away from our place called the "Señorita Esther private school." My mom had to pay a small fee for the services provided.

The small school was great. I quickly learned how to read and write and Miss Esther, my teacher, was very proud of how I picked up these basic skills. I rapidly went from a beginner reading book, Book I, to the much more advanced Book IV. I learned to read and write the Spanish language, which we never referred to as Spanish but as Castellano or Castilian. Miss Esther was a great and capable teacher. She continuously emphasized correct spelling exercises to ensure each student would never forget it, and she assigned older, more capable students to monitor children as they wrote misspelled words at least 50 times each until the correct spelling sank in. And, so it was, at the time I considered myself a good reader and writer. However, arithmetic and math were not emphasized at all, a weakness that came to affect me later in life. Arithmetic is the oldest, most basic and fundamental category in mathematics, involving basic calculations with numbers, such as addition, subtraction, multiplication and division.

A year later my mom enrolled me in the Escuela de San Victor, a Catholic Elementary School within easy walking distance about four to five blocks from our place, where I successfully completed second grade without a problem. Although Escuela de San Victor was managed by catholic brothers, the teachers were not catholic brothers or nuns but regular members of the community with some background in education. I felt that I did not learn as much as I did in the private school.

I was promoted to the third-grade level, where the elementary classroom was so crowded that it was almost impossible to learn anything. I estimate that about 50 to 60 children were piled at long, continuous school desks, each with separate draws. Because of my name, Rodriguez, I sat in the last row, which made things worse. The good students supposedly sat in the front of the class. The distance from my seat to where the teacher usually stood or sat behind his desk made it almost impossible for me to hear him. Add to that the background noise created by all the students and it was not the ideal school environment for learning. My teacher was a skinny old man with a mustache and spectacles that glided to the tip of his nose. He wore an old brown suit and had a squeaky voice. The man was a cruel teacher and the few times I was caught daydreaming, I was violently brought back by the teacher knocking on my head with his fist. Boy that hurt! Hitting children was allowed by the school administration and in general throughout the school system.

The year 1948 was critical for me and many other people throughout Colombia. Events occurred in my life that are difficult to erase from memory. Early that year, I made my First Communion. I attended many classes at the Escuela de San Victor, where a catholic brother prepared us for the rite. We learned that the First Holy Communion was a Christian ceremony held in the Latin Church tradition of the Catholic Church. That First Communion was to be considered one of the holiest and most important occasions of my Catholic life. It was when I received the Sacrament of the Holy Eucharist, the eating of consecrated bread and drinking of consecrated wine, for the first time. Catholics believe these rituals to represent the body and blood of Jesus Christ. Most Catholic children receive their First Communion when they are 7 or 8 years old because this is considered the age of reason. That was not my age when I had my first communion, I was almost ten years old. It was a memorable and beautiful day. My mother, being so religious, wanted it to be a wonderful day for me. She bought me new clothes, including shoes and a high quality, tailor-made black suit, as called for by the school. The school also sold us a white ribbon that was hung over my left shoulder and a bouquet of white lilies with a white candle emanating from its center, that you can see in the individual and group photographs. The two circles in the latter are around my mother and myself. The school hosted a small celebration with cake and a glass of soda not only for the grownups but for all the children who made their First Communion. I do not recall having many friends and neither did my mother, but we, in our small way, also celebrated my First Communion with a little cake and a special homemade dinner. I was happy that I was part of what I believed was my first party, first celebration, my First Communion. It was a beautiful day! After that, I could go every Sunday with my mother to the Candelaria church and take communion together during the 12 o'clock mass.

In third grade I found myself surrounded by a few bullies who picked on me by making fun of me and calling me names. I will never forget the day when I could not take it anymore and argued back with one of the regular bullies, calling him names. To me, he was a huge and fat bully, but to me all bullies seemed big. He challenged me to a fist fight after school. I had never had a single fist fight in my entire life. I was usually quiet by nature, but all the other kids were excited about the big fight scheduled for after school. The kids were selling tickets at reasonable prices, so I felt I was being railroaded into a fight I did not want. It seemed like the entire school was getting ready for the big match.

The after-school time arrived so fast that it was not funny to me, the main attraction. We met, stood up in front of each other and he threw the first and only punch. It was directed to my left eye and landed right on target. My classmates and other kids were screaming "Fight! Fight! Fight back!" He gave me such a powerful punch that my head flipped backwards. I saw bright multi-colored stars, as well as the moon and the planets and within a few seconds I started crying and running home to mommy. Within a few minutes, I had a black, swollen, closed eye. I could not see through that eye for a few days and, you can imagine, going back to school to face those kids was not an easy task either.

I was knocked out within a few seconds of the first round. However, I said to myself as a consolation statement, "I stood-up to him." My mom was very upset with me, of course, for getting myself in a fight with a "giant" as I described the size of the kid. She said, "Why don't you pick a kid of your own size." But he was my size! Or maybe he was even smaller, but faster with a sucker punch.

Chapter 3

The Revolution

COLOMBIA SUFFERED severely from a revolution that killed thousands of people. Prior to 1947, Colombia went through significant political unrest and on April 9, 1948, when I was just ten years old, a well-known and great political leader named Jorge Eliécer Gaitan was assassinated. Gaitan was a strong believer in gradual and peaceful change, balance between classes, land reform, moderate nationalism and a swing between Marxism and fascism. He rejected the idea of his country being led by the oligarchy and fought for the workers, farmers and the other minorities who had no voice in the building of the country. He had an oratory talent, reflected in his speeches that brought him unprecedented popularity. In one of his famous speeches, the political leader talked about two Colombian countries: the political country and the national country. This concept became a famous symbol for the Gaitan movement. Through his active participation in organizing many popular demonstrations, Gaitan managed to give power to social movements. Jorge Eliécer Gaitan was without doubt Colombia's most important political figure of the 20th century. Gaitan possessed an unmatched charisma which would have eventually taken him to the Presidency of Colombia. He felt the need for the implementation of comprehensive political reforms, adjusted to Colombia's situation at the time.

His early political activism emerged in 1918 when he supported the poet Guillermo Valencia in the presidential elections. A year later he was one of the main figures in protesting against the then president Marcos Fidel Suarez. As a result, he was very popular but also gained many enemies who preferred the status quo. A lawyer and intellectual of modest origins, Gaitan was a proponent of structural reforms and a fierce defender of the powerless. He graduated from Colombia's National University, where he wrote his thesis on *Socialist Ideas in Colombia*, demonstrating an early interest in left-wing political thought. He then studied in Italy, an experience which led to his rejection of fascism as a method which condemns rationalistic individualism of a liberal society and dissolution of social links to the social class that owns the means of producing wealth and is regarded as exploiting the working class. By the early 1930s Gaitan was already a well-known leader thanks to his ardent denunciation of the 'massacre of the banana plantations' in late 1928, where Colombian troops massacred thousands of workers demonstrating for better working conditions as later described by Garcia Marquez in his famous book, *One Hundred Years of Solitude*. Marquez won the Novel Prize in Literature in 1982 for his novels and short stories which reflected a continent's life and conflicts.

Gaitan then became Mayor of Bogotá in 1936 and was appointed Minister of Education in 1940. In both posts he

17

established social programs and public works which further enhanced his reputation as a defender of the poor. By the late 1940s Gaitan had become the unrivaled leader of the Liberal Party, transforming it from an elite-led party to one that began to channel popular desires for change, and which had majorities in both Congress and Senate. His platform was one that demanded "respect for the average person," that sought to build an economy "at the service of people" and to establish forms of participatory democracy as a way of ending what he called the "oligarchic regime."

Although portrayed as a populist leader, Gaitan had clearly thought out both his aims and his methods. His conception of the state was as "the synthesis of democracy," and he proposed the formation of a coalition that could agree on specific issues to advance the program of reforms. This alliance would have the dual benefits of avoiding "caciques" [chiefs] and violence. Gaitan did not believe in "catastrophic battles." He thought that Colombia, with its backward economic structures and its ignorant population needed generations to achieve profound changes. His economic thought was similarly developed: the economy was to achieve a balance of production and consumerism with a progressive abolition of exploitation and a state role in planning the economy and in redistributing wealth. "We are not enemies of wealth, but of poverty," he said, and he argued that in Colombia wealth could not be spread without a radical land reform program. He also proposed environmental legislation and labor laws, all within a transformative, revolutionary framework.

Despite his populist theatrics, this was not the program of a demagogue or dictator, but that of a democratic revolutionary, and was in many respects, like that of Salvador Allende in Chile. His vision and his vast popular support created many powerful enemies for Gaitan. The problem for his enemies was that within Colombia the landowning elites dreaded a potential land reform. Political elites also rejected his ideas on democracy and his anti-imperialist nationalism. In addition, Gaitan rose to prominence at a time when the United States was encouraging the closing down of democratic spaces across Latin America.

On April 9, 1948, Gaitan was gunned down as he left his office for lunch. While it is still unknown who was behind the assassination, the results were clear for all to see. His life was cut short and that changed the course of Colombian history, sparking massive violence and enabling elites to avoid having to make broad-based concessions.

Protesters started fires that destroyed many buildings, homes and stores during the revolution and many of my neighbors were intentionally murdered or killed by randomly fired bullets. Standing in front of my bedroom door, I could hear the horrible metallic ding made by those random bullets falling and jumping in the patio of my home. I was lucky that I was not hit. One day during this critical period, my mom left me alone at home. I walked to the front door of the huge house where we rented our room. I listened to the sounds of bullets razing everywhere. I approached quietly and carefully opened the heavy wooden colonial door. I partially opened one of the double entry hardwood doors and peaked from behind it. I was shocked to see a neighbor flat on the ground across the street, facing upwards and holding a few candles in his right hand. I later found out that his wife had sent him to buy some candles to light his dark room. I still can picture that unforgettable scene. There had been no electricity; the revolution fighters downed all the electric poles that served Candelaria and other parts of the city.

Trucks were loaded with what seemed like dozens of dead bodies stacked up one on top of another and taken to the cemetery where large holes had been dug to dispose of them in a common hole without investigating if anyone was still living. Many people who had gotten drunk on alcohol obtained from liquor stores that were broken into, had fallen asleep on the streets near dead protesters or casual bystanders. Their bodies were collected and buried alive; an event one cannot easily forget regardless of how many years go by.

Family members were missing, and search parties were organized to visit the Main Cemetery in search of loved ones. In some cases, the missing loved ones were never found dead or alive; in other cases, there were pleasant surprises when a missing member showed up at home unexpectedly. Often, individuals working far from home decided to stay with a friend or relative until calm returned to the city.

Since Gaitan's murder, Colombia has had a political system challenged by strong guerrilla movements. This has severely distorted Colombia's development, and has meant that Colombia, unlike the rest of the continent, has been unable to resolve its social conflict peaceably. After his assassination, Colombia succumbed to a ten-year (1948-1958) period of violence until Liberal and Conservative elites agreed to share power through a system of alternating the presidency between these two major political parties every four years as well as sharing the parliament. Other political forces were excluded. The violence also led to the creation of self-defense organizations by Liberal and Communist peasants. Many guerrillas who disarmed under a government amnesty in 1958 were killed, so therefore some decided instead to continue fighting.

Chapter 4

Convenience Store

IN MID-1948, sometime after the revolution ended and Colombia returned to almost a peaceful atmosphere, my mom sold the small milk business and bought a convenience store a few blocks away from the previous one. The store was a combination business and sleeping quarters. It had enough space for a double bed where we slept at night. It was a tight space without any closets or bathroom facilities, and we had to use the facilities of others to relieve ourselves. We took showers once a week, again, at a neighbor's home who had shower facilities in a "rooms for rent" property.

The dirty laundry we generated during the week was done as needed by a neighboring lady for a fee. That was the way to maintain a supply of clean clothes. There were no such things as washing machines or clothes dryers. We had no television; those who had it, had black and white only. Our small AM radio was the only means to get the latest news and soap operas. My mom loved soap operas. She listened to them daily, except on weekends when radio stations transmitted variety shows with comedians, singers, and miscellaneous groups playing typical Colombian music. She would listen to the popular ones of the day. She used to talk about each soap opera with neighbors and clientele; these were the only means of low-cost entertainment. She used to read novels such as The Three

Musketeers by Alexander Dumas and other popular novels
of that period.

My mom was a hard-working lady. Every day about
4:30 a.m. there was a knock on the door of the convenience
store. "Who is it?" she would scream, already knowing
who was outside. "El pan!" (The bread!), was the answer
from a young man carrying a huge basket on his back filled
with freshly baked bread for her to re-sell in the store. My
mom usually made the man wait for a while, as much as a
half-hour while she napped again until she opened the door
at 5 AM. The man of course had already laid the basket on
the ground and was leaning against the door, taking a nap
as well. There were no such things as a loaf of bread packed
in cellophane paper. To ensure that the delivery was in
accordance with what she had ordered, my mom counted
the assorted bread rolls, French buns, Italian bread and
other assorted baked goods which were warm and fresh,
ready for breakfast, lunch or dinner. She counted
everything one by one. If I were to compare those small
bread pieces to today's bread sizes, they looked like mini
Italian or French loaves. The fresh bread tasted delicious
and I was one of my mom's best customers. My mom
complained, saying I was eating the daily profits.

She derived all her income to sustain us from the
convenience store. In addition to the bread, she sold
general goods such as milk, sodas, flour, eggs, pencils,
miscellaneous drinks, candy, potato chips, daily local
newspapers and more to the neighboring community.

My mom had no education, but she was able to read, write and perform simple arithmetic functions. Her handwriting was horrible, but I could understand the notes she left me, so I could perform some chores for her. She and I slept in the store's back room and after the bread was delivered and counted, she would open the doors about 6:30 AM. The customers included almost every neighborhood family. A member would arrive early in the morning to buy bread, eggs and/or milk to prepare breakfast for the family's workers or school age children who had to leave soon. Refrigerators and freezers were considered luxury items that the community in general could not afford. That period was an "organic" period at its best; fresh meat, milk, fruits and vegetables were available everywhere. My mom was a good salesperson and throughout the day people stopped by to buy bread, cigarettes and other items. The store's closing time was usually around 10:00 PM, unless there were customers still inside the store; then she would close later.

There was one problem with the convenience store as I saw it: alcohol was sold without any government restrictions. Hard liquor, beer and wine were usually available during the day and evening. The sale of the beverages and drinks was a good source of revenue for my mom. However, when some customers had a few drinks they became rough. Their usual personalities changed, becoming abusive and vociferous as well as demanding additional alcohol when my mom refused to sell them anymore. Despite my young age and sleeping in the back room of the store, I interfered a few times to prevent things from getting out of hand. In general, most patrons and their friends were good people, only a few created problems by becoming obnoxious after a few drinks. I remember one night after my mom had already closed the store, a well-known neighborhood thug who was usually drunk started kicking the door and screaming obscenities, requesting that my mom open, so he could get more alcohol. I thanked the Almighty for protecting my mom against these individuals for so many years of store ownership. At the end of each day, after working an average of 16 hours, seven days a week, my mom was exhausted. She could not close the store on weekends because those were the most lucrative days of the week.

I know that my mom loved me very much and wanted the best for me, but she was also tough and rough at times. She built a whip with flexible thin strips of rubber, about twelve inches in length attached to a handle, especially designed to punish me whenever I misbehaved. She usually whipped me around my calves; she did not intend to cause bodily injury but pain only. It was painful, all right! I used to be dressed in shorts, and a few times my calves bled and had whip marks across them.

I was still attending the third grade at Escuela San Victor. I was not given any toys to play with so the only entertainment I had was to play soccer with the neighborhood kids. We played out in the street in front of the convenience store, using a rubber ball the size of a large orange. We organized two teams of about five kids each.

We used two stones or pieces of brick, placed about three feet apart to simulate soccer goal posts. The rubber ball had to go between the bricks to score a goal in such a short field. We ran back and forth chasing the ball until exhaustion and dehydration, often from sweating profusely, set in. There was no other place to play our almost nightly games. We were not allowed to go up the mountain, but even if we could there were no flat areas for a soccer match. What games we used to play! They were great! Those days and evenings were the best of my childhood.

Sometimes when we played very late at night under the dim street lights, my mom would sneak behind me and whack my legs with the whip, telling me that it was too late for me to be out on the street and ordering me to get back inside our room right away. It was dangerous because of the occasional vehicles going up or down the narrow street, which interrupted our game, making us split to safety on either side of street.

Chapter 5

Conceive Believe Achieve

I WAS A QUIET LITTLE boy who was many times scolded by my mom for not expressing my feelings, but when I did, my mom would say "Be quiet!" while she was talking to adult neighbors and customers. Children were not supposed to get involved in any conversations with grownups.

Dream is a metaphor for what you want to have in life; a good job, a loving relationship, wealth, health, travel or spiritual peace of mind. And one must be aware that the world has many options or paths to follow and finding their limits is by going beyond them into what appears the unachievable. At such a tender age, my conceived long-range plan was to travel north, perhaps a thought derived from reading El Peneca, a magazine designed for children and published in Chile that my mom used to get me occasionally. To convert that dream into reality seemed impossible, but it was nice to dream about it. Traveling north to me was getting out of Bogota and traveling to the northern part of Colombia, not understanding the potential dangers awaiting to a young person. Where could I go at such a young age? I could dream, and I did. To satisfy your long-range dreams, many steps are necessary to reach your main goal. The beginning of my traveling dream started at my mom's store. In addition to the Chilean magazine I read, my mom was given a map of Colombia by one of the store suppliers advertising miscellaneous products. The supplier stapled it on the most noticeable wall of the store where it could be seen by her customers. I used to look at that map and say to myself, "one day I will travel north from Bogota toward the cities of Cartagena and Barranquilla", both located on the Atlantic Coast.

"Born to Travel the World" is about sharing a unique case of self-motivation and determination. There could be similar accounts, with similar characteristics throughout the world but I feel that my story is unique.

My primary goal is to share with everyone that dreaming big is important and that with a strong will and motivation, one can achieve almost anything. I have been a dreamer since the early years of my life perhaps because of the circumstances around me that forced me to dream big or because I could not accept my mom's teachings, and those of my immediate environment.

Perseverance and positive attitude are key in achieving one's dreams. I never believed that it was easy to make dreams a reality. On the contrary. It is hard, it is fearful, it may cause anxiety, it is worrisome, and it takes work and dedication of many long hours or years of effective and productive work. It may include failures that must be overcome but one must continue moving along the dreamed path, the achievement path, until reaching one's short-term goals in search of the main goal; you then may pause, and look back and say, "I was there, so far away, and now I am here. What a good feeling that is. However, one can also say, "I am not there yet!" The route is long for the journey that I have chosen to complete, and it may take years to achieve that goal that seemed unachievable. However, one should not be concerned about how long it takes to get there. Worrying about it may discourage you from continuing traveling toward your dream destination. Rather, one must concentrate relentlessly on the ways to see the light at the end of the achievement path. It does not matter how many times you fall along the way but what is important is how many times one rises up successfully to victory, to complete the journey, to reflect and say "I am almost there! I am getting close! I can do it!" One can conceive it, believe it, and achieve it!

Chapter 6

Growing Up

CERRO OF MONSERRATE is one of the peaks with an altitude of 10,365 feet above sea level, in the mountain range flanking the city to the east and overlooking the savannah of Bogotá as it is usually referred to. It is recognizable by the church that crowns its top. The trees, plants, grass, wildflowers, and miscellaneous vegetation are always green all year round, and the scenery is just fabulous. The views of the city from the top of Monserrate and the peaks that surround it are incredible.

The Monserrate Mountain has been for many years a mecca for pilgrims due to the statue of the Fallen Christ, dating to the 1650s, and to which many miracles are attributed to. The history of Monserrate began in the 1620's to 1630's, when the Brotherhood of Vera Cruz began using the Monserrate's hilltop for religious celebrations. Devoted residents of Bogotá began participating in the climbing to the hilltop. In 1650, the founders decided to establish the hermitage retreat in the name of Monserrate's Morena Virgin giving the entire mountain the name Monserrate. By 1656 Father Rojas, manager of the sanctuary ordered a carving of a crucifix and a statue of Jesus Christ after being taken off the cross. The statue earned the name "El Señor Caído or the Fallen Lord." These sculptures were placed inside a small chapel dedicated to the adoration of Christ instead of being placed inside the religious hermitage retreat itself. Visitors to the sanctuary to see the statue of Jesus increased, rather than visiting the matron saint of Monserrate. By the 19th century, the "El Señor Caído" statue had gained so much attraction that the sculpture of the Virgin of Monserrate was removed as the center piece of the sanctuary and replaced with "El Señor Caído." The mountain has retained the name Monserrate to this day and for more than four centuries pilgrims and citizens have hiked the mountain to offer their prayers to the shrine of "El Señor Caído". The hill is a pilgrim destination, a tourist attraction, and a training ground for athletes and others wishing to keep themselves in good physical condition.

Visitors arriving to Bogotá, whether foreigners or Colombians coming from cities located at sea level, could be affected by the altitude even if they are fit. Fitness is irrelevant with altitude sickness. It is a mistake to think that if you are super fit and healthy that you will not be affected. Your body must maintain an adequate supply of blood oxygen levels to maintain adequate cell balances, and that is not within your control. Typical signs of altitude sickness are shortness of breath, slight nausea, and headaches. You must allow enough time to get to places, strolling not rushing. Carrying along with you a bottle of oxygen does help. Although there was a funicular tram used to reach the mountain top (a funicular tram is a transportation mode which uses a cable traction for pulling passenger vehicles on steep inclined slopes over tracks), many Catholics climbed up and down the mountain on their knees, and other times just walked up barefooted to pay tribute through self-punishment for favors rendered.

I used to climb the mountain walking, and/or jogging uphill, wearing tennis shoes, as my physical strength permitted. I usually went up and down on Sundays and occasionally Saturdays. I attended mass at the Monserrate Church and after the benediction, I ran down hill as fast as I could following the tortuous walking path while avoiding colliding with pilgrims flowing up or down the mountain. My entire body, shirt and pants were soaked in sweat, but I felt great after the physical exercise. Those were among the best days of my childhood!

At the end of that year I failed the third-grade elementary school, and my mom felt that I was dumb and therefore, I should start learning a trade, and that once I learned it, I could defend myself in life. I was about ten years old when I started earning a few pesos. A peso is the Colombian currency which at the time had an exchange rate of about 6 pesos per US$ 1.00. My first jobs included working as a messenger for a bookstore, as plumber's helper, and many other short-term trade jobs.

My mom felt that we had to take a vacation prior to my mom getting me working in a trade that would keep me busy all the time. She had never taking a break from her daily store chores, and she needed a rest away from it. She decided to take a week off from the store and closed it for a corresponding number of days to fulfill her personal dream of visiting the lovely city of Cali. Cali is a city in western Colombia, capital of the Department of Valle del

Cauca. It is the principal urban, cultural and economic site and one of the fastest growing economies in the country due to its geographic location. Cali's local climate is semi-tropical as the Western Mountain Range screens the flow of humidity from the Pacific coast towards the interior of the country. Due to its proximity to the equator there are no major seasonal variations and locals refer to the dry season as the city's "summer" in which temperatures can rise to between 93 °F to 97 °F and go down during the nights to 64 °F to 66 °F. My mom and I left for Cali by bus, a long trip with rough highway portions but we were sightseeing and enjoying the pretty scenery along the way. Once we arrived at our destination, we walked in the principal areas of the city and visited one tourist attraction after another, including a very popular church referred to as the Ermita Church.

We also went by bus to the seaport city of Buenaventura located on the Pacific coast. 90 percent of the population was of African origin. We had never been away from Bogota, and we enjoyed our trip very much. We returned to Bogota via bus and during the return trip all we did was to talk about how great the trip was and discussed details at length.

Colombia does not have the four seasons: summer, fall, winter, or spring, because of its location near the Equator. Anyone can travel within the country to any season they wish by car or airplane. Girardot city is home to several recreational spots and attracts many visitors from Bogotá. It is located at less than three hours' drive from the city and enjoys a tropical climate compared to the cold and rainy climate of Bogotá. It has an average temperature of 82 °F with a maximum of 100 °F. It is the second most important city of Cundinamarca State in accordance with its production. Visitors from Bogota travel on weekends or on vacation to this summer like city located at an altitude of about 1000 feet above sea level compared to Bogota's 8,612 feet, a significant drop from the capital city. One can also find winter like weather with snow and facilities for skiing in Sierra Nevada de Santa Marta, a separate area of the Andes, one of the most northerly mountain ranges in South America which makes for a beautiful view at a distance. There are no ski lifts to get skiers to the top, but it is possible for experienced ski mountaineers to hike up and ski down from the top. Traveling north to the cities of Cartagena and Santa Marta one will find summer temperatures all year around, beautiful beaches with fine white sand and other recreation facilities for one's entertainment.

I began to think about how to make my personal dream a reality that one day I would travel north. I never mentioned to my mother or anyone else my dream for fear they would think it was a ludicrous idea. I continued staring at that map of Colombia glued to one of the store walls searching for an answer and hoping that one day I would find a way to materialize it and start my travel plans. I kept thinking that I would go north, never south, always north, toward the city of Barranquilla located right on the Atlantic

Ocean coast. The estimated distance from Bogotá to Barranquilla was about 634 miles.

Chapter 7

Child Labor-Exploitation

IN MANY COUNTRIES children as young as four were employed in production factories, working long hours in dangerous, often fatal conditions. Children also worked as errand boys, shoe shining, selling matches, flowers and other cheap goods. Some children undertook work as **apprentices** working in miscellaneous trades such as manufacturing, construction, carpentry, plumbing or domestic service servants. Working hours were long, between 60 hours to 70 hours depending on the trade type. I was ten years old when my mom found me a job across the street from the store as a factory helper. This factory produced handmade silver products: serving trays, tea pots and cups sets, silverware, sports trophies, wine cups, glasses, bracelets, rings, and wristbands for ladies and men. What a job she got me into! I had no say whatsoever in the matter. "Out to a real job you go"! "she said," and start earning a living! No more school for you!" and so I did. Initially my responsibilities at the factory were to keep the place clean by sweeping the entire factory and to maintain cleanliness in the only bathroom available for about twenty-five employees. It was the practice for bathroom users to bring their own toilet paper or use old newspapers that were cut into square sections of about 5 x 5 inches that were hung on a wire-hook made from a clothes hanger and placed at one of the toilet's wall. To avoid clogging the toilet bowl, the used newspaper sections were thrown into a metal bucket for later removal.

As time went on, my responsibilities were augmented to assist skilled silversmith workers during the performance of their work. The company purchased many 6.25lb silver bars from the Colombian government for use in making the miscellaneous silver products. These bars had to be converted into pliable sheets of silver. This conversion called for melting the bars utilizing a smelting-furnace capable of reaching temperatures of about 1652 °F. I helped during the conversion of solid bars of silver to liquid silver (melted) and back to solid but smaller and lighter bars. I used to work near the furnace for many hours, under extreme heat conditions generated by the smelting-furnaces, and until the conversion process to smaller solid bars, sized 8 x 8 inches x ¼ inch in thickness, were produced. These lighter silver blocks were then machine pressed into long sheets of silver that were pliable enough to permit the silversmith specialists to cut them into circular shapes. These now thin silver circular shapes were referred to as discs of different diameters. The discs were then place on a metal lathe that rotated at high speed about an axis to generate various shapes as desired by the operator. The operator would slowly begin to reshape the discs into sections of jugs, pitchers, teacups, candelabras, water containers, tea pots, glasses, ornaments, and other forms. These sections were then assembled together by soldering its individual components to complete the final forms. Then all these products had to be polished with special paste that was applied either by hand or using rotating motorized brushes. As a helper, I learned to polish these products. I used to stand in front of a motor that rotated a 12-inch circular brush, which was used to polish the silver products until material impurities, scratches and imperfections were removed and a silver shined finish was obtained. I had to be careful in not getting tangled in the rotating brush which would have led to a serious injury. There was no such thing as life or health insurance that was provided by the owner in the event of an accident. The paste applied to the rotating brush rebounded back onto my clothes and onto my face and, despite using goggles, at the end of a given polishing job and after removing my goggles I looked like a dark gray scary monster. I used to take long showers while I scrubbed myself with soap and a pumice stone. After I got out of the shower, my mom would see me and ask me, "Did you take a shower?" "Yes, I did!" I replied. "You have circles of black dirt around your eyes", she would retort. "I am sorry mom, but that paste is not easy to remove". I was a victim of child-labor trafficking, although I was not forced through physical violence or threats to work in slave-like conditions. However, it was at my mother's wishes that I worked for this factory believing that a few years later I would appreciate what she did for me. I worked at this place since childhood and I ended up learning the trade, I became a skilled and productive silversmith capable of producing my own products. My wages were paid as a function of established per weight-unit prices and total quantities produced. Despite the hard-earned decent wages, I was not a happy young man. The long days, the accumulated dirt all over my overalls, hands, shoes, face, and head, made me think there must be a better way to earn a living. Yes, my head too, even though I used to wear a cap. In addition, there was always the potential for serious accidents resulting from the danger of being caught by the rotating axis of various motors or getting burned with gasoline while filling the gas tank of the blowtorch used for soldering the silver products. I saw a few accidents experienced by my coworkers that scared me all the time. One morning my coworker, also named Eduardo, was working on assembling by means of soldering silver components using a blowtorch when his blowtorch ran out of gas. He grabbed a pair of pliers and hit the gas tank's lid to unscrew it from the hot tank. The gasoline tank was filled at high pressure with flammable gas which upon unscrewing the lid, emanated from the tank spraying his face and neck, which caught fire immediately. With his face and neck in flames, Eduardo ran as fast as he could toward the toilet area where there was a large water tank filled with water. Eduardo jumped into this water tank extinguishing the flames from burning further his skin. He was rushed to the closest hospital where he remained for a few days. He healed completely but there were many scars left around his face and neck. I wanted out of such working conditions.

Chapter 8

New Arrival

MY MOM WAS a youngish pretty-looking lady, hardworking, with feelings just like anybody else, and despite having one twelve-year old son as her only companion for many years, she felt lonely many times. I noticed that when things did not go very well during the day, I would find her crying. My father had also been a failure to her and had never provided her with affection or companionship. He abandoned her when I was still a baby. I never met him except in photographs that my mother showed me occasionally. My mom was a single, respectable, and attractive lady with a strong character, and always had suitors after her. These men were from the neighborhood and usually married, irresponsible and rarely had good intentions of a serious and lasting relationship for my mom.

My mom eventually fell for a handsome man with blonde and wavy hair. I don't recall how they met, and since she had been on her own for many years, she hoped that this man who was not from the neighborhood might be her dreamed for companion. It turns out that he was not what she was hoping for. He was a compulsive gambler, already on his way to becoming an alcoholic, had a wife and other kids and one day stop showing up at my mom's. This short-term relationship between my mom and the "gambler" resulted in a new addition to the family, a handsome good-looking little brother with a very fair complexion. That addition increased my mom's survival problems. I could not explain how but she was so resilient and managed all adversity very well. The age difference between my brother and I was thirteen years. My mom baptized my brother Adolfo.

I was about fourteen years old and already working at the silver products factory and deeply involved in my work, when I heard behind me someone shouting my name and running toward my area of work. It was Arturo Cedeno, a neighbor, trying to tell me that my mom's store was on fire. I dropped what I was doing and ran back to the store. My brother was almost a year old at the time. When I got there, I could see the low-level flames rising dangerously in the back room. My mom was safely outside the store along with my little brother but in a panic. My mom had already sustained serious burns on her right leg.

My mom, in addition to attending mass every Sunday and praying the novenas used to light candles to the images of Virgin Mary and the Fallen Christ. The candles were placed on the cement floor, in front of the Saints images, and under the sink which was used to wash the dishes and silverware. My mom used to cook using a Coleman Two-Burner stove that used a gasoline tank attached to it to provide fuel for the stove burners. She usually kept the extra gasoline in a one-gallon container in the back room between the wooden shelves and the bed. The gas container apparently leaked gasoline, and although a few feet away from the candles, fumes from the spilled gasoline were ignited by the candlelight and turned into a flame which began rising dangerously. My mother noticed the rising flames and knowing that my brother was in the bed rushed to the back room and grabbed my brother and went out of the store onto the street. In trying to get my brother out of the back room, she stepped her right foot in the middle of the rising flames. This resulted in a serious leg burn for my mom. This action may have taken a few seconds. I was simultaneously running back to the store and I arrived within one minute, I rushed to the back room with the flames still rising, grabbed the bed blankets and dropped them on the flames to suffocate them, preventing what could have been a serious fire. All ended well except for my mother's burned calf muscle on her right leg. There was a nurse living next door and she treated my mom's leg for about three months. There was significant scar tissue left on the right calf of her leg.

My mother decided that we needed additional space not only for me but for my brother too. She rented one single bedroom in a house two doors away from the store. The house was built to make rooms available to small families or single persons that could not afford to rent a large apartment or purchase a condominium or small home. These rental homes included 10 to 12 rooms where tenants share a single bathroom with a shower and a toilet and a second bathroom with just a toilet. It was difficult to take a shower on weekends due to the lines of tenants wishing to get cleaned up for the following week. There were many times when a tenant was taking a shower and second toilet was being used by another tenant and a third tenant wanted to use the toilet or take a shower and was not able to. The tenants were working people consisting of husband and wife where only the husband worked making low wages while the other was responsible for their children, if any. These were the living conditions of the poor working class.

Chapter 9

Teenager Days

I WAS WORKING on a trade since childhood, a trade that I hated but for which I was getting pay. I had become an average silversmith; it was a trade that would allow me to survive on my own as my mom wanted. Was I happy? No, I was not! My mom always advised me to select friends that were better educated than I was, were not bullies, and had good habits. If you could learn something good from a friend that would make you a better person, do so, good habits are important. She would tell me, "Be honest and stay out of trouble". My best friends were Rafael, Marco, and Horacio; Rafael was the oldest, Horacio was next, and the youngest was Marco. The families of these three friends were homeowners with the financial resources to enroll them in private schools. In terms of education they were ahead of me and getting further away as time went on. I was fortunate that I got along well with them, and that I was invited to some of their parties. However, I felt that I was out of place most of the time. When I was introduced to their friends, girlfriends, and family members I was not comfortable. I was not able to maintain an intelligent conversation. They felt that I had a nice personality and worked hard at Rafael's family factory of silver products. I was not too happy about it. I began to realize that I was considered handsome but dumb, and, therefore, snubbed many times especially by the young ladies which were in search of a better catch. That was my secret of course.

Marco considered himself ugly due to the shape of his jaw, and his close friends gave him the nickname of "pepa de mango", or mango-seed. His friends were cruel and hurtful, disregarding his feelings. I did not think that was appropriate or nice of others to call him by his nickname, and I never called him that. In my opinion he was a great and smart guy.

Marco, who was also bound for college, used to play chess. I thought that he could teach me to play the game during my spare time. The game of chess was always associated with a game that was played by kings, maharajahs and in general for the middle and upper class. Chess is played by a diverse range of people and ages for many different reasons; they enjoy the companionship it offers, the skill and logical thinking it involves, it can be played anywhere, it is fun, extremely challenging, and at times, frustrating. Playing chess allows you to make new friends and meet interesting people. You are never alone if you can play the game. It is said to improve thinking skills; it can help you find a solution to a problem that you felt did not have one, and to get your thoughts under control. The game of chess seems to have originated in India 1,500 years ago before the 6th century AD. Then it was brought to Persia where it was played by the Muslim world and subsequently to Southern Europe. In the second half of the 19th century, modern chess tournament play began, and the first World Chess Championship was held in 1886. The game consists of two armies fighting against each other represented by the pieces that evolved into the modern pawn, knight, bishop, rook and queen, respectively. The final objective is to capture the opposing army's king,

Marco started teaching me to play the game on Saturdays and Sundays when we did not have much to do. I became so fascinated with such an interesting game that I was determined to improve my game skills by playing with others. I looked for a place where others were playing chess. There were a few coffee shops in downtown Bogota that had dedicated playing areas with corresponding chess tables that included the chess board, and one could rent the chess pieces and a table on a per hour basis. Both players would pay for the rental. It was inexpensive, there was no need to buy alcohol and, on the average, you would find that there were great people to play with. I began meeting interesting players of all ages that played the game very well. I usually lost all the games I played but I did not care nor was I discouraged because despite losing many games I enjoyed the game and I was learning every time a new move. I was becoming a better player as time went on to the point that I began winning here and there and soon started beating Marco. Playing and improving my game became my favorite pastime.

Mr. Cabrera was a men-suits designer for main stores in Bogotá, and who was well known in the neighborhood. He used to tailor only men's suits using the highest quality material for men's ware. He was a one-man team who was kind enough to assist me in selecting and purchasing material to make me a good-looking suit. He spent time taking me to various stores where material was sold at wholesale prices. I selected the material and color and he would tailor me a suit based on my specific design characteristics in accordance with what was in fashion at the time, and at a reasonable price. I loved to dress up around my birthday: tailored suit, white shirt, fancy tie, new shoes.

The custom of dressing up perhaps was derived from my mother who began dressing me up since I was a little boy with brand new clothes every year on the date of my birthday. She dressed me up and then she would take me to have a professional photographer take my picture. That tradition started when I was one year old and continued until after my First Communion. I never had a birthday party or heard of my neighbors and friends celebrating their birthdays. There were some people that had no idea or remembered the date they were born.

We, as young teenagers, became friends with the Frazier sisters, three sisters about our age. They were pretty, each having different personalities, but they had good and clean habits, and best of all were authentic. We used to go to their place to visit. We organized miscellaneous group competitive salon games where penalties were awarded to the losers. We had fun, laughing and playing till late evening hours. I recalled losing a game where my penalty was to be dressed up as a girl wearing makeup and lipstick. One of the girls brought me into another room, put some makeup on my face and young ladies' clothes. I did look like a female and when I walked back into the room all laughed hysterically. Everyone had a good time. All games were clean. No foul language or alcohol was used.

At one of our parties, I danced with the middle sister to the tune of slow music, closely tight to each other. It was nice, my first experience with being so close to a girl. She was smart and started liking me. However, I could not mislead her. I was not ready for any relationship. I did not have the heart to take advantage of her. I also acknowledged that I was timid, and uncomfortable in the company of others, an anomaly perhaps caused by the work I performed and lack of education. I had no subjects or themes that I could discuss or share with the educated that would make some sense. I had one good attribute. I was not shy when I told dirty jokes and short stories that I had learned from customers that gathered around to have a few beers at my mom's store, and from my coworkers while working as a silversmith. I was popular and discovered that I could keep a group of friends under my control by the number of dirty jokes I shared and for which I had the ability to mimic the characters in the joke while expressing details to their amusement. Should I become a comedian? No, I could not, I told myself. I must get a better education. But how? I did not like my job but what else could I do? I wanted to travel but how? There must be an honest way to convert my dream into a reality. I was invited to many parties by my friends Marco and Horacio, I did not have the ability to sing or play any instrument, but I could dance and used to love dancing and welcomed invitations to dancing parties. The following photographs depict moments of my childhood, first communion and teenager days and my mom and little brother.

Childhood-First Communion and Youth

Dress for Birthday Photographs   My Childhood Street

My First Communion At Escuela de San Victor

My brother and mother
on Bogota Streets

My teenager years and my tailor-made suits

50

Monserrate Mountain and Church

Monserrate Mountain - Altitude Of 10,365 Feet

Pilgrims attending mass at the Fallen Christ Church in Monserrate Mountain

Chapter 10

General Rojas Pinilla

L A VIOLENCIA WAS now in its tenth-year, 1958, a period of civil war in Colombia between the Conservative and the Liberal Parties whose respective supporters fought most battles in the rural areas. "La Violencia" was considered to have begun with the April 9, 1948, assassination of the politician Jorge Eliecer Gaitan who was a popular Liberal Party candidate set to run for the presidential election in November 1949. His political murder provoked the "Bogotazo" rioting that lasted for ten hours and killed some 5,000 people. An alternative historical perspective of La Violencia proposed 1946 as the start of the violence, the year when the Conservatives returned to government power; when rural town police and political leaders encouraged conservative-supporting peasants to seize the agricultural lands of liberal-supporting peasants, which provoked peasant-to-peasant violence throughout Colombia; a civil war for control of the country's agricultural land. "La Violencia" is estimated to have cost the lives of at least 200,000 people.

In 1936, General Gustavo Rojas Pinilla, a civil engineer, graduated from Tri-State University, a private non-profit post-secondary institution located in Angola, Indiana, United States. As a civil engineer, he participated in the engineering, design and construction of highways and other works as part of his military career. He was later sent to the United States to acquire weapons and other machinery for the Colombian Armed Forces. In 1944, he became assistant director of the School of War and in 1945 Director of Civil Aeronautics. It was there where he presented his project for airports in Colombia under the name "Landing Tracks in Colombia," which served as a dissertation for his promotion to colonel in the Army. Landing Tracks became a reality with the erection of El Dorado Airport and other airports during his presidency. Rojas became a Colombian Army General who led a coup d'état in June 13, 1953. The National Constitutional Assembly recognized and appointed General Rojas as legitimate and constitutional President of Colombia. He was elected President of Colombia in 1954.

On June 13, 1953 when I was almost 16 years old and had been working as a silversmith apprentice since I was a child, my friend Rafael, started knocking and screaming on my bedroom door; "Get up! Get up! General Rojas has taken over the entire country! he said. I replied, "What are you talking about?" I was somewhat concerned. While I was getting dress, he explained, "General Rojas was the Chief of Staff of the Armed Forces of Colombia under President Roberto Urdaneta Arbelaez and he has seized power by means of a successful coup d'état against the incumbent President Laureano Gomes Castro and supported by both liberals and conservative's parties." Rafael said, "We have to go down to the Bolivar Square and join the rest of the population in welcoming the General's coup d'état. He did it for the benefit of our country", he said.

I got dressed as fast as I could and together, we walked about six blocks from our street down to Carrera Septima (Seventh Avenue) to join the huge crowds of people supporting the takeover of the country's highest office. We climbed on power distribution electric steel poles and screamed loud and clear "Viva Rojas Pinilla", repeatedly, along with the rest of his supporters. We followed the multitude that was getting larger by the minute as it was approaching the Bolivar Square along 7th Avenue.

I followed my friend's lead in the overall Rojas Pinilla celebrations. I was screaming because I heard others screaming with all their might. I had never heard of Rojas Pinilla, but it was fun. We returned home during the evening after having my first expression of political support for someone that I had never heard of. We had hoarse throats because of the shouting, and we could hardly talk. Most of the time I was working almost nine to ten hours a day. On Saturdays after I finished work, I took a shower, wore clean clothes, had lunch at my mother's, and walked to the downtown café to find someone to play chess or play a game of billiard. There was always another player of my strength to play with. Sundays, I used to climb to the Monserrate Mountain, by foot, of course, attended mass at Señor Caído Church, ran back down the mountain as fast I could, arriving drenched in sweat. What a good feeling that was. There were many occasions that my mom and I went

54

to mass on Sundays to fulfill our religious beliefs. The following Monday I started my routine of working five and half days per week

.

Chapter 11

My Best Friends

R AFAEL'S FATHER, referred to as Don Pedro, was the owner of various jewelry stores in central Bogota that sold expensive diamonds, emeralds, 18 carat gold chains and rings, men and ladies wrist watches and products produced by the silversmith factory I worked for. He was wealthy, a good man, a man with a golden heart. Rafael also had two other younger brothers, Pedro, and Juan the youngest. All attended well known and exclusive schools in Bogota. Their two-story home was across the street from my mother's store, and on the second floor Don Pedro and his family lived and on the first floor the silversmith factory was located.

Rafael continued talking about the solution to the many problems affecting Colombia. My friend Rafael, enrolled by his family as a cadet at a military school, the Colegio Militar Cooperativo, used to wear a military uniform and a beret. He looked "cool" and was very proud of his uniform. At times, I wished that my mom had had the means to send me to a military academy so that we both could be wearing such a cool uniform.

We were about the same age, and he was very familiar with the Colombian government and the people's political and violence problems affecting our democratic institutions. It seems to me now that that period was the peak of disarray of Colombian political parties and the quiet but explosive civil rural war that had continued since the assassination of Jorge E Gaitan in 1948. He was aware of the rural areas civil war between Liberal and Conservative landlords that were fighting to secure a larger piece of land ownership.

Rafael had been attending the best schools right from childhood in an organized fashion with the strong support of his affluent family. He also benefited from family discussions at dinner time that were about politics, the government and/or about the impact of the civil war in rural areas upon the overall economy of Colombia.

I, on the other hand, was uneducated, and a laborer at his father's factory. We were good friends and the difference of our families' wealth had no impact in our relationship. On weekends we met as two young friends and shared individual values in our respective worlds. We went to the movies, played pool, and spent time together talking till late and, of course, we discussed girls. We went to or organized many parties using the home of those that were permitted to use their living rooms to have a party. Some friends knew others that could play musical instruments; there was a DJ who owned equipment that consisted of a set of speakers and a record player used for entertainment at parties. The DJ friend derived income from these events. These were all the friends that usually spent time together with us.

LOUIS RODRIGUEZ

I considered myself an introverted person when meeting others that I respected as educated. I felt embarrassed when certain important issues were discussed, and I was not able to respond or participate intelligently. I felt mortified and awkward but never guilty that I had only third grade level education compared to most of my friends. At times, I felt jealousy and envy of what they had but I understood why I could not or did not have it. I loved to go to parties because I loved to dance and considered myself a good dancer. However, when I found a nice girl that corresponded to my dancing abilities, she was disappointed any time I opened my mouth. Although I was polite, she danced with someone else at the first opportunity.

As advised by my mom, "Select your friends, don't just be around anybody", and so I did. My second-best friend, Horacio was enrolled in the Colombian Military School of Cadets, a school that was established to meet Colombian's need to develop cadets that would eventually become officers in the Colombian Army. Cadets had the option to become civil engineers, lawyers, business administrators and physical education instructors which allowed them to follow a career in the military. My two best friends had gone away to follow paths that would either lead to careers in the military or in the civilian life which would make them useful individuals to society, themselves, and their families.

Horacio was very proud of attending a military academy and wore a nice-looking cadet uniform, very

58

colorful, elegant, and imposing. The uniform consisted of a green jacket with golden buttons, bright red collar tied around the neck and light blue pants with black shoes. The uniform included a cap with a flat sloping crown, band, and peak (visor), used by many military organizations throughout the world

I was at Horacio's home, when he started showing me his uniform that was laying over his bed. Sensing my admiration for his uniform, and perhaps my wishes of wearing something similar, he quickly said, "Here, take the jacket. Wear it to see what you look like". I was reluctant to do so since it would make me sad thinking that I could never attend a military academy. I did try it on, and I thought that I really looked good.

Horacio lived in a small two-story home which his family owned. The family occupied the second floor which included a small size living room. The first floor was rented as a large convenience store with quarters for the tenants to sleep in. We used to organize parties at his place with the permission of his parents. Each friend contributed something to the party, food, light alcoholic and soda beverages. We always controlled the intake of alcohol, never drank in excess, and were responsible for our acts. There was never a fight or arguments, always clean dancing and fun.

I was about 17 years old when coworkers about the same age felt that we should play billiards and drink a few beers. I had learned to play billiards, an indoor game, which used a felt-tipped stick to hit one ball out of three balls across a cloth-covered table. One ball was of color red, the other two were white, but one of the whites had a black dot to differentiate them from each other. The billiard tables were available almost everywhere throughout the Barrio as the main entertainment for the young and the old.

This night, after playing a few billiard games at the Café Panamericano, located about a block away from the Plaza de Bolivar, my coworkers and I, as agreed, had a few beers. A few beers were enough to get me drunk, and unable to walk straight. I knew where I was and where my home was, and I thought that I just better go home. I started climbing the 12th street hill toward my place. An older fellow from the neighborhood who recognized me while I was stumbling left and right up the street, grabbed me by one arm and eventually dropped me at the store at about 11 pm.

My mom was waiting for me outside the store concerned and upset that something had happened to me. At that time, I was already much taller than my mom and growing up fast. She stood up on top of a small wooden stool and started smacking me over my head and shoulders with a broom and wherever she could land that broom on me. I found out the next morning what happened the previous late evening. I could not remember clearly what had happened that night, but what I did feel was the headache, a continuous shivering and desire to throw up, not a good physical status to be in. "Mommy, I am sick! I said". I am dying with a terrible headache! What do I do! I am thirsty too! "She responded." "Who told you to get drunk?" "Mom help!" "And she said, "suffer the consequences!" I learned the hard way what hangovers were all about. My mom had no mercy with me; no aspirin, a glass of orange juice, or a succulent well done steak. In those days having chicken was a luxury and when we had it, it was on special occasions only. I could have meat almost every day because it was affordable compared to chicken. My mom never had a drink of alcohol. After that experience, I do not recall getting drunk again to the point of losing control of my behavior.

Chapter 12

The Castro Sisters

ILMA AND LYLIA, the daughters of a successful owner of a hardware store in downtown Bogota, were referred to as the Castro sisters. Marco's parents were also owners of a hardware store located across the street from Ilma and Lylia's store. The sisters and Marco had a relationship of many years, since childhood. In 1954 I met Lylia, a 19-year-old young lady for which we had something in common, we both loved dancing. Lylia was already a high school teacher, who loved to dance to the tune of our Colombian music, and she was great at it. We were both invited to a dance party at a mutual friend's home not too far away from my place. We danced together most of the evening. After that night, in 1954, Lylia and I never saw each other again until four years later. She used to live in Barrio 20 de Julio, located about ten miles away from Barrio Candelaria. The only way for me to get to her place was either by bus or an expensive taxi ride. We did not exchange phone numbers or plan to see each other again. Marco was always flirting with the idea of making Ilma his girlfriend and was never successful. Ilma was never responsive to Marco's seduction attempts. Marco suffered in silence Ilma's disdain for what he believed was a profound love for her. He kept his love for Ilma in a silence mode for many years until he unlocked the vault of silence and shared his feelings with us. Ilma was pretty, had a beautiful smile, an upper lip that was very attractive to many, and was also a good dancer and very witty. Ilma liked Marco but not as a boyfriend. She had a boyfriend and Marco learned the hard way to accept the reality, anticipating that nothing was going to happen between Ilma and him. Marco invited Lylia and Ilma to various parties organized by Horacio, or another friend, and these get-together events were usually held at different homes. Marco brought the sisters to each party via taxi from the Barrio 20 de Julio.

The two sisters, when invited to parties, did not go without the other. When Lylia and I met that night in 1954, that party was just like any other one. The home hosting the party prepared dinner, provided a music system, and guests danced all night, usually until about 4:00 a.m. of the next morning.

I did not see Lylia until about four years later (1958) when she was 22 years old, and I was 20. Marco invited the two sisters to various parties where dancing was the main purpose and, of course, to be around mutual friends, an activity we shared dearly. Lylia and I danced with each other and as the days and weeks went by, we began to like each other increasingly. I felt that she had big and pretty eyes, a beautiful body, a body which she highlighted by wearing tight skirts or dresses that were glued to her skin outlining all her body curves to any man's fascination. At one of this these parties, we began talking about a date later. She was educated and was continuing educating herself further in various other ways.

In my effort to show off my best skills, and perhaps my only one, dancing, not only to her but to those that were attending the gathering that evening, I attempted to make a dancing step referred to as "la tijera" (the scissor). "La tijera" consisted of a person jumping up in the air, spreading his/her legs wide open, one leg moving forward while the other one was moving backwards, then reaching the floor while the legs were still wide open and immediately bouncing back to a regular upright position. While I was trying my "cool" step, I slipped and fell flat on my back in a thunderous way. Wham! The entire second floor of a two-story family home trembled under the weight of my body. Everyone turned around to see my "cool" dancing step, a complete misunderstanding, or better yet a disaster. I fell! There was not one person extending me an arm to help me to get off the floor because it was felt that was part of my dancing routine. I was in pain, but I quickly got off the wooden floor and continued my dancing. The people thought that was my special "cool step" for the night and started clapping. Clapping! While I was flat on the wooden floor!

Lylia and I exchanged ideas and talked about our respective backgrounds, desires, plans, family members and educations and experiences. I described what I was doing at the time with some details such as the type of work, lack of schooling, how filthy I would get daily, and my dissatisfaction with my inability to do better. There was nothing to worry about, she said. And added "You are not happy with your job, but you are earning a living through working hard." The only good thing about my job was that I received reasonable wages for what I did. I never shared with others my dissatisfaction with my job. I was earning a salary and I was saving as much as I could, which was a good habit of mine. She hinted that there was no reason for me to be concerned, that she did not care much for my educational background or the type of work I did but what she liked about me was that I was a hard-working person. We began a relationship, dating frequently, and eventually I was taking the bus to her parents' home at Barrio 20 de Julio, and coming home to Barrio Candelaria, late at night, about a 45 minutes ride.

Lylia, in addition to be an elementary school teacher, used to take ballet dancing lessons and studied languages; Italian, French, and English. She knew some classical music, read books, and had some singing ability. Her family had adequate financial means, they owned a hardware store in downtown Bogotá and a large home with many rooms for rent. She occasionally managed the main hardware store. What a match!

I was desperate to get educated. My mother was not helpful either feeling that I should keep working as a silversmith. I found out that having two years of elementary school and reading and writing well I could take bookkeeping courses to become a bookkeeper and later an accountant. I had nothing to lose, and I started taken night courses at the popular Cosmo Bookkeeping

School. There were schools that did not care whether you qualified or not. If you could pay the tuition fees, you were accepted. That was the beginning of my night school attendance while I was still working as a silversmith. I completed one semester which included the submission of bookkeeping books for a fictitious business owner. I used to sit at my mom's bed facing the back wall which had a built-in cupboard with various shelves without doors. I did my bookkeeping homework on the lower shelf which became the equivalent of a desk.

My homework consisted of balancing all ledgers. All the work had to be done using hand-calculators since regular computers had not been invented yet. I did not have a typewriter either, and my bookkeeping books had to be written with a pen. Smudges of any kind were not accepted. My regular income dropped since I could not work as many hours and my wages were on a commission basis on items produced. After six months, I submitted a set of bookkeeping books, well balanced and ready for the review and grading by the school faculty, and I never heard from them again. They claimed that the set of bookkeeping books were not found. I was defenseless and unable to fight back. I quit that career path. What a waste of my time and money!

My friend Roberto, also from my neighborhood, and I used to lift weights to build strong and well-defined bodies. He recommended that I should take English classes. He was studying English at the Instituto Colombo Americano and thought that English would be an asset for both of us for a better future. My girlfriend Lylia was already taking English classes at the same school. "Why not?" I said. There was no specific reason to justify taking any English classes except that it was trendy at the time and I could also brag about my ability to speak another language. Listening to Lylia and Roberto individually about how much they were learning, I became interested in learning English. I found the location of the Instituto Colombo-Americano's and visited the registration office, enrolled, and began studying English.

I was amazed how quickly I began to learn the language. I learned basic grammar, writing, pronunciation and understood uncomplicated sentences when spoken to. I followed the recommended sequence of courses. One of my coworkers who had a brother working at an airline and knew I was taking English classes asked me; "Hey, how do you pronounce this word?" He wrote "Airways" on a piece of paper? I had never seen such a word, and by just reviewing the spelling, I was able to pronounce it correctly to his satisfaction. He said, "Very well, that's it. My brother taught me how to pronounce it."

Understanding the native English speakers was very difficult for me. I had American teachers, both men and women, for every English class but it takes time for your brain to adapt before one can say, "I understood what he/she said". Your brain must get used to the new sounds. That was the hardest part of learning a language. It takes time.

I did not need English in the type of work I was doing, and I had no idea why I was taking English classes except that perhaps it could help me later in life. It was a good feeling to acknowledge that I knew some English. I thought, I could get a job with an international airline company as a host whose job was to greet and help airplane or cruise ship passengers. However, knowing English was not enough. Additional education on many other subjects was a necessity. I wanted to get away from that adequate paying job, but literally dirty and hard labor work I was doing. I did continue studying English at night at the Instituto Colombo Americano. I used to come home late, but I felt it was worth it. There was the possibility of changing my current job for a better job.

Lylia was also studying Italian at the Instituto Italo-Colombian. She invited me to the Colombo-Italian Institute to an evening of piano recital by a famous Italian maestro. I slept like a baby for most of the piano concert, despite Lylia's elbow nudging into my rib cage. She told me that those attending the recital could not concentrate in listening to the cultural and sublime recital. "It was fantastic!" someone said, and others said, "What a harmonious recital, what a concert!" I said to myself, "great sleeping music," I slept through the entire recital. And, I was noisy with my snoring. Lylia referred to it as the roaring of a lion combined with whistling sounds that created a jungle atmosphere with the audience requesting; "Miss, can you tape his mouth, we want to hear the pianist." She never took me again to classical music concerts. I used to work long hours as a silversmith, so it was possible that I was tired all the time and I would take any opportunity I had to nap and, of course, I could really sleep to the sounds of a piano playing, unintentionally. An embarrassing situation!

My daily activities for the next two years became a routine, work during the day and studying English at night. I was highly motivated to find a new job opportunity which was cleaner and with a better future.

Chapter 13

The Dream

I FELT THE PRESSURE of a girl that wanted to have a serious relationship leading to a wedding. She purchased a bedroom set and other items to furnish an apartment or at least to have a furnished bedroom; I was not ready for a commitment! I would have not been able to support a wife and children. I appreciated what she had done but the fear of getting married, having children, and working to sustain a family drove me to a serious decision, stop the relationship. We had a fight which led to the ending of our relationship. I panicked! And the relationship with Lylia was over.

I met my friend Horacio by chance in downtown Bogota with Avenida Jimenez, and Carrera Septima, who was on vacation from the Military School of Cadets. We talked, as friends usually talked, exchanging ideas, and discussing girlfriends and the like. At one point during the conversation he mentioned that he would be traveling to the USA soon. I do not recall why he wanted to go to the USA but that did not make any difference to me. When he said that, sparks illuminated my brain, and I said, without any hesitation and not knowing what I was about to get into, "Me too! How do I do that?" I asked. He said, go visit the PILOTUR Travel Agency, located on Jimenez Avenue and ask for Señor Pilonieta, the Agency owner. He will help you.

I rushed the next day to investigate my options to travel to the USA. I met Mr. Pilonieta who indicated he would help me. After completing many forms and paying a fee, all of it done through the travel Agent, I began to wait anxiously for the approval of the application as the initial step. Horacio went back to his military duties and never saw him again.

I continued my daily activities, working, taking English classes, playing chess, and being with my friends. Time was slowly passing waiting for the issuance of the United States visa. Toward the end of the second half of 1960, I unexpectedly ran into Lylia, my ex-girlfriend, in downtown Bogota. She was walking along the Carrera Septima near Jimenez Avenue without any defined direction, or so it seemed to me. We talked, reconciled and the relationship started again. However, I explained to her that I was trying to get a resident's visa to the USA and that I was hoping to depart for the USA within months.

There was one specific document that was considered very important. Mr. Pilonieta drafted a declaration of facts letter to be signed and notarized by someone in the United States stating that I would not be alone while in the USA, and that I would be provided guidance, and financial support as may be needed. The letter was written in its final form, I mailed it to Eduardo, who resided in New York, and whom I knew for several years. It seems that initially he was reluctant to sign it. A second letter had to be written and mailed back to him. He signed it in front of a Public Notary who duly stamped and signed it authenticating his signature and Eduardo sent it back to me. Mr. Pilonieta submitted that letter almost immediately to the American Embassy.

A few months later, around September 1960, after running back and forth with additional documents to satisfy the American Embassy requests, I was scheduled for an interview. I met a Visa Section American Consul Lady who asked me many questions. I remember one question in particular; "What are you going to do in the States?" She said. I answered without any hesitation whatsoever, "I want to work and study."

Toward the end of October 1960, I did get my residence documents enclosed in an Embassy sealed yellow manila envelope to be hand-carried for delivery to the Immigration Officer at the port of entry in the USA. I, alone in my room, jumped up and down in celebration of my initial step toward traveling north to the land of opportunity. Enclosed in the yellow envelope were my visa documents and outside the envelope there was an Embassy Letter of transmittal stating that I had four months to depart Colombia in route to the United States. I have never been a person that brags about any successes until the success materializes. I started building my wardrobe in preparation for my expected departure to the USA. In addition, not knowing what my initial economic conditions would be in the USA, I was saving as much money as I could to purchase my airline ticket, and to bring with me enough cash to hopefully last me for some time. I was also limited by my suitcase size as to how many personal items I could carry.

I began to share with my close friends that I was departing soon for the USA. A few laughed at me right at my face without mercy. My coworkers knew that I was just like them, uneducated silversmiths working to make ends meet and that I was living at "Mom's Hotel". "You! You are going to the United States?" one said. "Don't make me laugh!" "You don't have a visa; it will never happen!" Those were some of the comments I heard. That hurt; however, I did not try to convince anybody or share that I had a visa and that I would be leaving for the USA within a few weeks. In a similar manner my failures, if any, were always my secrets. I had no hard feelings against anyone.

My mother could have helped me financially, but she never offered to do so. I bought my one-way airline ticket for US$350.00 and I was left with approximately US$450. My grandmother gave me 500 pesos, about US$84. This amount combined with the cost of the airline ticket was my entire savings. When I started working as a silversmith helper my initial salary was the equivalent of $6.00 per week, or about US$1.00 per day. In terms of Colombian pesos, my per week salary was 36 pesos. This low salary increased as time went on and I learned the silversmith trade. However, it was still a very low salary in relation to what one may call decent trade wages.

The owner of the travel agency suggested the conversion of the Colombian pesos, that were left after paying for my airfare and land transportation cost, to US dollars at the prevailing exchange rate. I agreed, he gave me US$ 150.00 in cash and a check for US$ 300.00 to carry with me. I had no bank accounts, credit cards and/or check books of any kind. I learned to save money early in life while taking advantage that I was living at my mother's home where food, rent, laundry and other miscellaneous expenses were provided by my mom. I was responsible for paying for my appearance such as suits, shirts, socks and shoes and minor weekend expenditures such as playing chess, billiard or going to the movies with friends. I was able, after personal expenses, to save the money for my trip. I used to save my money in a drawer of a four-drawer wooden chest that my mother had the local carpenter make for me, and where I used to keep my clothes and other belongings.

The initial phase of my childhood dream had begun to materialize. Breaking away from my dear mom and my little brother, my girlfriend Lylia, and my best friends, getting a USA visa, and paying for my airfare to NYC, were important steps. I was on my way!

Part Two

New York City-Army Days

Chapter 14

Departure to the USA

THE THOUGHT of getting on an airplane for the first time was giving me an uneasy feeling. Perhaps the combination of getting on a plane, traveling away from my mother, and going to an unfamiliar land created a feeling of uncertainty. I was unwavering and felt ready to meet the challenges of the unknown. The travel package included three days in Miami where I would be given a short tour of the city by a local representative from the Travel Agency. Then he would take me to the Greyhound bus terminal to continue my trip to New York City (NYC).

I was then 23 years old when the moment for my departure arrived. It was January 1961 when my mother, my little brother Adolfo, and I, arrived at El Dorado Airport. There were one or two of my mother's neighbors, and a few of my friends that went to the El Dorado Airport to wish me farewell. My best friends Rafael, Marco, and Horacio could not come due to their college duties that conflicted with my departure date and time. I was used to dressing well and wore my best suit and tie and dark blue wool coat. As I climbed the stairs of the aircraft to board the plane, I turned back with sadness and waved my hand to everyone that came to see me off, especially towards my mother and brother. I knew my mother would feel my absence the most. Her suffering would be unbearable for some time until her acceptance of my departure and understanding that perhaps it was for my benefit would settle in. I was the older son, the one she would share with some of her happy moments when we both laughed, and when together resolve customer problems, and neighbors' gossiping issues. My brother was still young, almost 10 years old, and I felt that he could serve as a companion to my mom.

People were asking me prior to my departure, "When are you coming back?" I was just leaving and had no idea when my return would be. At that time, returning to Colombia was not part of my long-range plan. There were many other issues such the hope of educating myself even though I was beginning to get old.

My trip went well and in accordance with the travel plan. I saw important tourist attractions of Miami such as the huge mansion of the wealthy Esther Jane Williams, the then famous swimmer who had set multiple national and regional swimming records while in her late teens and who later became a movie actress working for the Metro-Goldwyn-Mayer company. All this was new and exciting for me. I had never seen the beauty of the blue and wavy ocean waters, its white and fine sand beaches, people walking in casual wear: shorts, khaki pants, sleeveless shirts or in swimming suits. The tall palm trees and the three or four lane highways crisscrossing the city of Miami amazed me. I felt like I was in wonderland. There were so many new things to see and admired compared to my Barrio Candelaria.

I had written a letter to my friend Eduardo, letting him know of my arrival date and time. We never spent time together, he was older than I was, and he had been manager of the silversmith factory. That was basically our relationship. Eduardo agreed to pick me up at the Greyhound bus terminal on the day of my arrival. I boarded the Greyhound bus toward the great city of New York, a 30-hour trip with occasional rest stops. The bus trip was rather uneventful with only a minor incident when we were crossing the state of Georgia and the bus had a rest stop in the city of Atlanta. I was approached by a stranger dressed in a suit and tie and speaking Spanish who requested that I show him an identification which I did and there was no problem. I assumed that he was an undercover agent from the immigration services agency. Eventually we arrived at the Greyhound Bus Terminal in NYC.

I got off the bus, grabbed my suitcases and started looking for my friend. I had arranged with Eduardo to pick me up at the bus terminal. I did not see him anywhere. I was loaded with bags containing my personal items and other items given to me by others in the hope that I could generate business for them. There was a neighborhood carpenter that designed and built acoustic guitars. He built a special guitar made from the hard shell of an Armadillo. Although it was smaller than a regular acoustic guitar, it was bulky, and it had to be carried by hand.

I was waiting at the 34th Street Greyhound bus station along with many other passengers. It was crowded, people were moving in all directions, and at times colliding against each other and saying, "Excuse me, excuse me, sorry, so sorry." Those apologetic statements were the magic words that would prevent the people's collisions from getting out of hand and into serious arguments.

I waited, and waited, and waited and after over an hour and half I decided to search for his phone number. I called Eduardo a few times, but no one answered his phone. I knew that he lived somewhere in Queens County, but I had no idea how to get there nor did I have his address. I was given one of his friend's telephone numbers, German Rodriguez, who lived in Manhattan. I called him, and thank God, someone answered the phone. German did answer the phone, and I explained my situation. He asked where I was, and I responded that I was at the 34th Street Greyhound bus station. He understood and asked me not to move from where I was.

He arrived, and I end up staying at his apartment located on Amsterdam Avenue and 84th Street, Manhattan. Later that evening I phoned my friend. He was at home. He told me that he had been waiting for me at the bus station and that I had never arrived. I told him that I was there sitting in the middle of the bus station where I could be seen by anybody. "Where were you?" I asked. He told me that he had been waiting at the 42nd Street bus terminal. I said that I was at the 34th Street bus station, the last bus stop. Then he said to my amazement; "That is not the last stop!

The last stop is 42nd Street. No wonder I could not find you. You got off the bus at the wrong bus station."

German seemed like a nice person, round face, bushy hair, and Colombian also. He was working at a small toys' factory in Jamaica, Queens called Brillium Corporation. The factory produced plastic toys day and night. German usually worked the night shift, the reason I found him home when I called during the day. A week went by in suspense, expecting for something to happen but nothing, really nothing happened, except that I found a Savings Bank within a short distance of the apartment and I opened a savings account and deposited the $300.00 check along with some cash that I had, the first bank account that I ever had. The travel agency in Bogota had issued the $300 check.

German was subletting a small space at that apartment which was rented by Carlos, also Colombian, and a good friend of Eduardo. Eduardo had discussed my arrival with Carlos and agreed that Carlos could sublet me a portion of the apartment. Carlos usually rented the entire place to as many people as he could fit in the apartment. The apartment was of the railroad type. The term "railroad apartment" describes a lay-out that is like that of a typical passenger train car. Such cars had compartments located along a narrow corridor running along the entire car length. Each compartment may include a bed or two seats, one in front of the other for passengers to share. Carlos' apartment had three rooms along the corridor that were accessible from a hallway that ran the length of the apartment from the front door to the back room. I had to share one of the rooms with German.

The apartment included two medium size bedrooms, one bathroom, a kitchen, and a small living room. My new friend German talked to Carlos regarding renting me a room or a portion of a room. Carlos had already three additional sub-tenants living in his apartment, two sisters and German for a total of four. I would be the fifth sub-tenant. We all shared one toilet, a shower and kitchen on a first come first served basis. The ladies when using the bathroom facilities took forever to get out of the bathroom.

German told me that he was going to talk to his manager regarding a position for me. My first few nights at my new quarters were not the best. I was not able to sleep. I was not used to the unbelievable street noises coming from the neighborhood streets. I could hear sirens blasting away in unison from police cars and fire department trucks and loud music, singing and/or screaming from neighborhood bars and community people. I had to get used to this nightly activity if I wanted to sleep all night.

I had never been exposed to the winter season: snow, freezing temperatures, and heavy wind and slippery street conditions. I had never lived in an apartment that was heated via a steam system with radiators located at key places throughout the apartment. The apartment was always hot, very hot. I blamed the heating system for three boils that emanated on my rear end and on my right thigh to be exact. This happened during the first few weeks after my arrival to NYC while living at Carlos apartment. I was attending some night English classes at a Public School not too far from the 82nd Street apartment.

At the public school, I met a nice and mature lady from Puerto Rico, and I told her about the boils that were growing out of control. She told me that she was living with an older man from the Philippines whose background was in nursing and perhaps he could help me out. I went with her to see him at their place. He looked at each of the three boils and told me they were getting infected. The man had a First Aid Kit with enough items to work on each of my boils.

The boil area over time, became firm, hard, and then increasingly tender, subsequently, the center of the boil softens and becomes filled with infection-fighting white blood cells from the bloodstream to eradicate the infection. This collection of white blood cells, bacteria, and proteins is known as pus. This pus had to be removed carefully. In his First Aid Kit he had among other things: bandages in a variety of different sizes and shapes, small, medium, and large sterile gauze dressings, safety pins, tweezers, scissors, cleansing wipes, sticky tape, antiseptic cream, painkillers, cough medicine, antihistamine tablets, distilled water for cleaning wounds. He had it all.

He started by wiping the boil area with the alcohol-free cleaning wipes, followed by wrapping the tip of the tweezers with cleaning gauze. He then began removing the pus. The tweezer and gauze went deeper and deeper into a hole about 1 inch deep with a diameter of less than ¼ inch created by the infected boil. He changed the gauze and ensured the wound was very clean. He added a disinfectant and filled up the hole with gauze allowing a short piece to stick out. He worked in a similar manner on the other two boils. I was concerned with the depth of the boils and the potential for a serious infection affecting my health. However, after a few more visits to the Philippine nurse to clean the wounds and change bandages, the boils healed within a few days. I was very thankful of the male nurse that worked and healed them.

Chapter 15

First US Jobs

ERMAN SAID the Brillium Floor Manager would like to interview me the following Monday. I was pleased at the possibility of getting a job. German had told me that American food was very nutritious and that for breakfast I should have only a bowl of cereal or a cup of coffee and a slice of toasted bread. That would be enough for an entire day.

I was used to having about five meals daily which included a homemade breakfast prepared by my mom before leaving for work (7:30 AM), a small sandwich and a soda sent by my mom to the factory during the morning work - break (9:30 AM), my regular lunch-hour was about 1:00 PM. I used to go home to have a lunch that included a nourishing bowl of soup and a plate filled with portions of potatoes, rice, beans or peas and/or carrots and small portion of meat. Then around 3:00 p.m. she used to send me small salami and cheese sandwich to have during my work-break. At dinner time I had basically a repeat of what I had for lunch. Although we belonged to the under-privileged community, and we had no dining room table, there was always food available for us. I used to work hard, performed physical exercise, climbed the mountain, and in general was very active and therefore, was not overweight but healthy prior to my arrival to NYC, despite that I was overfed growing up with food which consisted of carbohydrates and miscellaneous fats.

I went to the factory on Monday with German for an interview with the manager. I got up early in the morning, took a shower, selected my best Colombian tailor-made suit, matching shirt, and tie, and got all dressed up for my interview with the Manager at the toy company. It was still winter and was a very cold day, I decided to wear something warm and I wore my Colombian tailor-made wool overcoat. I felt that I was well dressed, looked smart and hoped to get a decent job regardless of my educational background. I followed German's lead in getting on and off trains on our way to the factory, located in Jamaica, Queens. We boarded one train at the 82nd Street Station toward midtown Times Square Station where we changed for another going toward Queens County. We got off at the 74th Street in Queens and changed once again for an underground train toward Jamaica Queens, our destination. We walked a few blocks, arriving on time to talk to the Manager.

It did not take too long for the Manager to offer me a job. I spoke to him with an accent but in well-structured sentences. I managed to understand him because I studied English in Colombia for about a year or more. However, my hearing comprehension was not ready yet for the New York accent. It was difficult for me to understand anyone unless he/she spoke very slow. The Manager told me that I would work forty hours per week for a total salary of

$40.00. My take-home pay was about $25 per week. I could not understand why but I had a job, which was great! and German was working there too.

I was told by the manager that my responsibilities would include among others to sweep, mop, and in general clean up the entire premises, including the ladies' and men's bathrooms. In addition, I had to pick up and return cardboard boxes back to their original place. The manager also said: "Make sure that when you report to work next Monday you will wear working clothes. Forget about a suit, white shirt and tie, shiny shoes, etc..". I replied, "I will do that."

Most of the employees were women working along a conveyor belt consisting of a flat surface with a sliding belt stretched over the top. The belt had enough tension to move freely and it was connected to a set of wheels, at either end, which rotated the belt around the flat surface. The Foreman or his assistant would bring large cardboard boxes containing small plastic parts and/or metallic pieces that were used in assembling the miscellaneous toys manufactured at the factory. A box with miscellaneous parts was placed alongside each lady, and each lady was responsible for assembling together a specific section of the selected toy for production.

Early mornings all the ladies lined up along the conveyor belt to get ready to begin assembling toys. The conveyor was energized and began rotating without any toy parts on it. The needed parts had been located already in boxes near each lady prior to the opening time of the company by dedicated employees that arrived early morning. At the beginning of the conveyor belt there were only toy parts ready to be assembled into toys and when the conveyor belt reached the other end, a toy was born. It could have been a doll, a truck, a gun, or other toy of the many that were designed and produced by the company. As time went on, I began to assume other responsibilities such as organizing the industrial shelving racks where the individual cardboard boxes were kept containing the individual pieces that made up the toys.

These racks that occupied the larger section of the floor space, were used to accommodate the entire company's inventory of individual components used in assembling the miscellaneous toys. This inventory was kept in a complete disarray throughout the facility. There were boxes all over the floor laying near the metallic racks. These boxes should have been organized in the existing racks way above the ground. I learned to use the forklift and when I had time, I started working in organizing the entire inventory. In a few weeks the existing physical inventory of miscellaneous parts was completely reorganized to the best of my knowledge with boxes labeled and in corresponding racks. One of the Managers invited the company owners to show them what a nice job he had "directed". I did not mind, I was treated with respect and getting a reputation of being a good worker.

Chapter 16

Girl Friend

I RECEIVED A LETTER from Lylia letting me know that she would be arriving in NYC sometime in July. Surprise! Surprise! When I left Colombia there were no plans for her to travel to the USA. I did care for Lylia and I welcomed her arrival. I had to move out of Carlos' apartment in Manhattan since he could not accommodate anybody else. I found a family, through my friend Eduardo, that owned a two-family home in Woodside, Queens. The place was closer to the factory where I was working at the time.

The family was Colombian, consisting of a husband, Daniel, and his wife, Libya, and five children. Daniel's family derived additional income from renting available space, just like many other homeowners did when there was only one family member working who was not earning enough income to cover all home expenses. If space was not available, they created it. In this case, Daniel, a hardworking person, was responsible for the home mortgage payments, car payments, heating and ventilation, electricity, water and of course food supplies. They had to rent the first floor and rent any other space available on the second floor to make ends meet. They owned a nice home, but they lived under crowded and tight economic conditions, keeping an eye out that expenses did not exceed total income.

They rented me a space in one room which had two beds and I shared the shower, bathroom, and kitchen facilities with the owners. The conditions at this place were much better compared to those at Carlos' place in Manhattan. The neighborhood in Woodside was also great, no police and fire trucks blowing sirens, drunken and noisy individuals emanating from bars down the street, cars honking, etc. Also, the distance to the toy factory was shorter and I could leave from my new place later, and still arrive at my workplace on time. In the afternoons, after finishing my workday, I would also arrive back home earlier.

While I was working at the toy factory, I met a coworker whose origins were from India. We talked almost every day at lunch time which allowed me to begin practicing my English comprehension through a direct contact with an English-speaking person, although his accent was not of a native New Yorker. He was from India. I made every effort to stay away from Spanish speakers without offending anyone. Many of the employees were from Cuba and Puerto Rico or from Central or South America just like me, and therefore, Spanish was spoken among ourselves. I was in a hurry to learn English. I felt that without the proper communication skills it would be very difficult to get a better job.

The toy company was subdivided into a few production departments and my Hindu coworker was a supervisor of one of them. I had about four months on the job when one day my Hindu friend told me he was selling his car, a car that was about four years old at the time. He owned a 1957 Ford sedan. I had no idea why I decided that I could afford to buy the car. I could not drive and therefore I had no driver's license. My take home pay was about $25 per week. The price of the car was within the amount of cash available in my savings account, about $300.00, the amount I brought from Colombia.

He asked me if I could drive and I said yes. He took me out for a ride to make sure I liked the car. I had never sat in front of a car's steering wheel in my life. He sat on the passenger seat and told me to start driving. I am sure he noticed I was not trained to drive a car, but he was eager to sell me his car and he took a chance by allowing me to drive it. Initially I drove without a problem until he said, "let us get on to the highway", which we did. I was swerving the car left and right very dangerously. "Oh God! What am I doing?" And all I could hear from him was a loud and clear scream "Louie, Louie, Louie" repeating my name many times. I managed to drive the car to the side of the road to a full stop. I gave him back the car. I must say that I was very fortunate that I did not cause an accident, and that a traffic police officer did not see us. I stubbornly bought the car! As it turned out later, what a mistake that was!

I was not able to drive it because I had no driver's license. My Colombian friend Eduardo, as per my request, registered the car under his name, which he should have never done due to the risk involved, a young person who never drove any type of vehicle, and through him I got car insurance as the initial step. I got the documents to study for the written examination to get my Learners Permit. I took the written exam and obtained my Learner's Permit. I still was not able to drive my car unless I was accompanied by a licensed driver seating at my right on the passenger's seat. I was driving without a driver's license from my home in Queens to my place of work and back to my home in the evening, which was not a good idea.

Lylia arrived as promised during the month of July. She had no problem getting a Visa to the USA. Their family provided the financial assistance to show the American Embassy that she had some financial strength to travel to the USA on a tourist Visa. The Visa was good for six months.

I had already requested to the family where I was staying to see if they could accommodate Lylia to which they quickly responded "Yes, of course". It was a place to sleep, take showers and with access to the kitchen for frying eggs, boiling water for a hot chocolate, and do minor cooking, and we could use the refrigerator to store juice and milk. Lylia's arrival meant additional income for Daniel and Libya regardless of whether they had space available or not. She moved in to live with us in the same house where I was living.

It was not clear how German found out about the Woodside place and he asked for rental space for him. He moved in to live with all of us including the owner's five children. The total number of people in that second floor of a two-family home was now 10. German worked at night and I worked during the day. A few days later I got Lylia a job at the same factory.

In accordance with the rules stated in my entry documents to the USA, it was my responsibility to report to the USA Armed Forces Office for a 2-year tour of duty within six months of my arrival to the USA. And so, I did! The subsequent step was for the Army to let me know when I had to report to take the physical and intelligence examinations in accordance with preliminary induction procedures.

I was driving with Lylia through my old neighborhood on a Saturday afternoon in midtown Manhattan. She was sitting at my right-hand on the passenger's seat of my recently acquired 1957 Ford, when I noticed through the rearview mirror that my car's trunk gate was open. I stopped, got out of my car and closed it. Then out of nowhere a police officer walked over toward me to ask for my driver's license, registration and car insurance. I had two out of the three items requested. I did not have a driver's license. I had a Learner's Permit issued by the NYC Motor Vehicle Department. I had taken successfully the written test and I could drive if I were accompanied by a duly licensed driver which my girlfriend sitting on the passenger seat was not. Big, big mistake!!

I was given a $50.00 traffic violation ticket and was told that I had to go in person to the Police Department Traffic Violation Bureau to pay for the ticket. I was working at the toy factory full time during the day and I preferred not to miss a day's work. I had also registered at a private night school to learn English. I was in a hurry to improve my reading, writing, speaking, and comprehension abilities of the language. I had a busy daily schedule.

German was working the night shifts, and I asked him if he could go to the Traffic Violation Bureau to pay for the traffic ticket. He replied, "Yes, I can do that." I assumed that because he had been in this country for more than two years, had time during the day, knew the city well, and how to get around it in terms of transportation, he could help me out. He should have had no problem whatsoever paying for the traffic violation. He agreed to help. I went to my Savings Account Bank, withdrew the cash and I gave him the $50.00 to pay for the fine which was more than my $25.00 take home pay salary, and I did not worry about that traffic ticket anymore.

I continued working at the factory as usual, making my daily trips to the toy factory in Jamaica and back to Woodside. This became a daily routine activity along with my attendance to night school to take English classes except for the weekends where I had some free time after completing homework assignments.

Another month had gone by when the manager at the toy factory called me into his office, closed the door, and asked me, "Are you in trouble? And I said, "Of course not. Why do you ask?" He said that he had received a phone call from a detective from the police department asking questions about me. What! I panicked; I had no idea what was going on. The manager gave me a phone number to call this person.

I called to find out what happened, and I was told that I did not report to the police department as required by the issuance of a traffic violation ticket. German never went to the Traffic Violation Bureau to pay for the ticket.

I confronted German about it, and he explained that he had gone to the place, and that the line was too long, and that someone volunteered to pay the ticket on his behalf. He gave me back the ticket without any official stamp that would have indicated payment. Nor did he return the $50.00. I told him that we both had to go to court to explain to the court what supposedly happened.

German brought along his uncle who spoke English well. The Court also appointed a public defender to help me out. He gave the judge the same story since neither German nor I spoke English well and the judge believed us. German's uncle also spoke to the judge on our behalf explaining the confusion. The judge ruled that although he felt bad about what had happened, he had to impose a penalty. That penalty was that I had to pay the fine again which I did. I lost an additional $50.00. As far as I was concerned, German was not able to go the Traffic Violation Bureau for whatever reason. His English was weak, and perhaps not being able to find out how to get there, as time went by, he decided to keep the money and hope that everything would be ok with time.

Chapter 17

The Army

GERMAN'S RECOMMENDED diet of a bowl of cereal and one toasted slice of bread daily had not worked well. I lost so much weight after six months that I thought I looked like a toothpick. I was very skinny.

I started looking for another job and found one working for a company that manufactured electronic components designed for government defense projects. I had worked for the toy factory for about six months and I felt it was time to find a better job. Once I started the new job, the company provided me with on-the-job training to become a wiring-person. The job was in accordance with my level of education, but I liked it; the pay was higher, and the type of work compared to the previous one, "broom and mop" services, was better." I would never regret having worked for a company as a cleaner. On the contrary, I had to start somewhere, I needed to practice my English as much as possible and learn slang sentences from my coworkers. That was my starting up point and I appreciated it.

Starting in 1948 through 1973 young men in the United States were drafted to fill vacancies in the armed forces which could not be filled through voluntary means during both peacetime and conflict periods. The Selective Service and the registration requirement for America's young men served as a backup system to provide workforce to the U.S. Armed Forces. The Selective Training and Service Act of 1940 was signed by President Franklin Roosevelt which created the country's first peacetime draft and formally established the Selective Service System as an independent Federal agency. I arrived at the United States during the early 1960s, at age 23, and it was my responsibility to register in the US Armed Forces Selective Training and Service within six months of my arrival to the USA.

A few weeks went by at my new job when I received a letter from the USA Armed Forces with a request to report to the Army Induction Center in downtown Manhattan. I was under the age of 26 and it was my responsibility to serve in the US Armed Forces. I had no choice but to report for army duty. I was being drafted into the Army subject to passing my physical examination and a background check.

I reported to the Induction Center located in downtown Manhattan as required for my physical examination and to undertake a series of written tests. These written tests would determine my intelligence quotient (IQ) and my education level which would allow the Army to determine where I would serve the Army best. The initial forms that were completed called for the reporting of any problems with the law. I was, of course, clean except for my traffic violation which I reported without any hesitation or any intention of getting away with not serving in the US Army.

I welcomed the opportunity to serve in the Army as the means to better myself in many ways. Learn English and begin night school to improve my education level. I saw the Army as an initial steppingstone to a better future. I knew that I would be a better individual once I served my two-year Army duty. I saw the two-year draft as a personal training program to a better and lasting future. I would be bilingual, Spanish and English, to begin with.

I learned later that a bilingual career was a very competitive field since there were millions of people that were bilingual throughout the United States. In many cases many people spoke three or more languages and they provided translation services at no cost while getting pay for performing other duties. Professional translation services are well-defined services where one may derive a decent salary when working for international organizations. The United Nations use these translators to translate orally and written documents from one language into another language. I was not looking for that type of work. I was just dreaming of traveling the world.

In the induction forms I completed for the army, I reported the traffic ticket incident and I was told the Army needed to investigate me further to make sure I didn't have a police record in addition to that traffic ticket. My induction was delayed for some time. I was supposed to hear from the Army later with their findings regarding my qualifications for duty. I received a letter about five months later from the Induction Center stating that I was to report with my belongings to the Battery Park Induction Center located in downtown Manhattan. The Army had found me qualified, without any criminal records, or legal violations of any kind, to serve a two-year tour of duty.

The call to Army duty generated another personal situation related to my girlfriend Lylia. I did love her and could not just walk away from her again. We talked, and we decided to have a civil wedding. We had no family members in the US, no close friends either nor did we have enough funds to organize a simple reception to celebrate the wedding. We collected the documentation needed to have a civil marriage conducted by a representative from the court and proceeded to get it done. We secured one witness and got married on January 1962. The wedding took place at a Court in the County of Queens, NY.

There was no wedding cake, maiden of honor, guests, banquet, or band playing the nuptial entrance song. It was just plain and simple. The wedding was not intended to get away from serving in the Armed Forces. on the contrary, it allowed me to bring my wife with me once I reached my final army post. The Army welcomed service men that were married, and therefore, could bring their wives along to their permanent post of duty. The married men were supposed to provide stability to the army and had the potential to extend their service duty reducing the number of trained soldiers leaving the armed forces. The army liked that, of course!

Another problem that had to be resolved prior to joining the army. What to do with my 1957 Ford. I had used the $300 in my savings account as a collateral to borrow the money needed to buy the car. I was given a booklet that included coupons where each coupon stated the amount to be paid each month over a two-year period. I had to find a buyer as soon as possible since I was not able to take the car with me as long as I was in training. I spoke to Daniel, the owner of the home in Woodside where I was staying. I made it attractive to him by suggesting that he did not have to give me any cash just take over the monthly payments included in the Bank's booklet. Thank God! He did agree. I was now basically ready to report for duty at the time and place indicated, February 1962, at the NYC Induction Center.

I went to the Induction Center as instructed on the date and time indicated. There were many other inductees along with me. I was given a complete physical examination, a battery of tests to determine my education level, and I was on my way to loading the buses toward Fort Dix, New Jersey. I arrived at Fort Dix to start my two months Basic Training and upon completion we would be given certificates stating that we were now soldiers.

All the trainees reported to the barber shop during the initial week for a standard army haircut, a crew cut. We exchanged our civilian clothes for green army fatigues, two pairs of army boots, three sets of T-shirts and a package of underwear. Civilian clothes would never be used again except while on leave; the army green fatigues were my

99

new dress code. The weeks I spent as an Army trainee were a nightmare due to my lack of understanding of oral English. The sergeant in charge of our basic training spoke very fast, in a slang, and most of the time he was always shouting which made him incomprehensible from my viewpoint.

Rather than saying "I don't understand you", and I knew he did not care, I decided that I would imitate others as much as possible when commands were given. One early morning the sergeant in charge brought the entire platoon out in formation and everyone knew that if he gave the command 'Jump" to someone, that person would jump as high as possible. I was thinking that the moment the training sergeant stood up in front of me, and he screamed something incomprehensible I would jump too because I was mimicking the soldier before me who was performing jumping jacks.

One time when the basic training sergeant screamed at one of the trainees and I saw that he started running around the barracks until he completed twenty laps. I got ready to do likewise when the sergeant stood up in front of me. He screamed in a similar manner and I thought he wanted me to do the same. Before he finished his sentence, I started running around the barracks. I continued running until I completed about twenty laps, and then reported back to my spot within the platoon. This sergeant noticed what I did, and he appeared very upset.

I had no idea what the problem was, until he started screaming out of control right on my face. Then another

Spanish speaking trainee translated for me what he was saying. He said, "Drop and give me twenty pushups" which was the initial command he was yelling at me before I started running around the barracks. I was exhausted from running twenty laps around the barracks. I was obviously out of shape. Not just me but all of us, new arrivals were in the same conditions. I obediently and quiet dropped to the ground and gave him as many pushups as I could. Many felt that it was funny, but I did not think so.

There were also many embarrassing situations such as when one of my new Hispanic friends asked me in Spanish if I wanted to have something to eat at the post's delicatessen. I said, "Yes, Of course, let's go". He further told me that he would let me place the order, so I could practice speaking English. He said in Spanish "Ordene para mi un sandwich de queso y una coca cola" that is, "Order for me a cheese sandwich and a coke." I said, "Ok." Then I said to the young lady. "Miss, I want one shit sandwich and a cock." the lady stared at my Hispanic friend and they both laughed hysterically. My friend translated what I had just said. I was very embarrassed and thought it was not funny. I felt the need to accelerate my ability to speak English and improve my comprehension when I was spoken to. It was still a long way for me to become proficient in all four areas; writing, reading, speaking, and comprehending the English language.

The next step in my trip during my Army tour of duty and after completing a two-month Basic Training at Fort Dix New Jersey was to wait for my next assignment.

Everyone was eager to know where they would go next. A few would be going overseas, others to various Forts throughout the US. I was given my orders which stated that I was to report to Fort Gordon, Georgia, for an Advance Infantry Training.

I did report for training at Fort Gordon after taking a few days off. I completed my training at Fort Gordon, and I had a choice to re-enlist for another three years with an option to be stationed in Germany, Okinawa, or any other US Army post in the world that might be available for enlisted men duty. The "Enlisted men" expression was used to refer to those individuals that volunteered for army duty. In my case, I was not enlisted. I was drafted. It was my obligation to serve in any US armed forces for a period not to exceed two years. The enlistees usually served a minimum of a three-year period. If I had volunteered, while on duty, I would have had to serve an additional three years for a total of five years of army duty, a strategy that was not on my horizon. I could not see myself serving additional time in the army. I was not planning to give up my independence by traveling to another country where most of the time I would be stationed at an army post and perhaps having weekends off only. I would have to follow orders from any Army person that had one stripe above my rank. When the sergeant, corporal or anyone with an extra stripe would shout "Get down! Get up! Clean here! "Drop and give me so many pushups or run around the barracks twenty times," I had no choice but to follow orders as established by the Army rules and regulations. No Way!

That was not for me. I would complete the two-year draft duty, leave the Army with an Honorable Discharge and start a civilian life.

At Fort Gordon I learned what discrimination against members of the black race was all about. I had noticed that in Miami, but I did not make too much out of it. I noticed that public bathrooms were divided into two types, bathrooms for the white race and bathrooms for the black race. Each bathroom type had corresponding signs painted at the entrance to ensure observance by the users. No one had brought this to my attention or talked to me about it nor I had heard about it while in Colombia, I had just observed the prevailing situation.

At Fort Gordon as part of our training activities we had to go on bivouac or military field training exercises to simulate guerrilla warfare. We were moved in trucks and were dropped at designated training camps. We were provided with warfare gear, weapons, water canteen, carried extra socks, etc. We took long walks, walking at a fast pace and usually for hours without stopping for a break. We walked at times on a single file, one man behind the other, along dirt roads, through dense forests. It could be at night or daytime and we could be away from our main post for days or weeks. We crossed rivers as needed to meet warfare training objectives.

I enjoyed the entire effort except during the winter season. Our training activities took us to the State of South Carolina many times. There was a bivouac routine training during the summertime when after many hours of fast walking, loaded with our respective gear, the platoon sergeant decided that we had enough that day and we loaded the trucks back to the post. The platoon leader decided that we should take a break, and we did stop the truck near a supermarket before getting back to our post.

Everyone was getting off the truck. I was next to the last in getting off, and as I was proceeding to jump off the truck, I noticed a black soldier still sitting down on the truck. I said, "Let's go", to which he replied, "I can't". I said, "Why not? No money? I have some". He pointed at his face with his index finger, indicating that I should look at the color of his skin, black. He appeared so sad and resigned to accept the race discrimination that was affecting the southeastern part of the country, and replied, "I am black, I am not allowed inside that store." I felt sad and offered to bring back something for him to which he responded, "That is OK. Don't worry about it." Everyone came back to the truck and we continued our trip back home.

Another incident that I recalled as if it had happened yesterday, is that during my training exercises at Fort Gordon, Georgia, members of my Platoon were sitting on the ground in rows one behind the other forming a large rectangular shape about 32 x 64 feet empty space. The training sergeant began calling pairs of soldiers to engage in a fight against each other simulating hand to hand combat using a tool equivalent to a rifle. Each soldier had to hold with both hands a three feet long wooden stick having a diameter of about two and one-half inches and at each end the equivalent of 16-ounces boxing gloves used by boxers during training sessions. The idea was to simulate a rifle with an attached bayonet and use it as a weapon to defend yourself or attack an enemy soldier during an actual war. The combined rifle and attached bayonet were weapons of importance for infantry attacks as a weapon of last resort during hand to hand combat. In this regard, it was used as a supplementary close-quarter combat weapon.

The wooden stick with its corresponding boxing gloves without thumbs was a training tool used by pairs of soldiers, selected at random to exchange blows against each other in a friendly way until one or the other got upset. I was sitting in the second row among the rest of the squad, and the training sergeant said, "You, get up, you are next", I was not expecting it, nor did I want to fight anybody, but it was my turn. I got up, and a huge tall Afro American soldier was my opponent. I saw muscles everywhere throughout his body, and he had a height of at least six feet three inches compared to my five feet, eleven inches. I thought that he was lean and mean. We both were in excellent physical condition based on the continuous physical training. We were each given the long stick with boxing gloves at each end, and when the sergeant gave the command "fight" we had to start smacking each other till we were told to stop. My opponent and I started fighting against each other. I was gentle when I stretched my arm to hit him on one side then on the other side of his body. Then suddenly he started hitting me without any mercy until my anger started bubbling up. This rage was a normal response to what I believe was a dangerous threat. I became furious to the point that I was uncontrollable. I started fighting, smacking him left and right relentless while he was retreating, and I kept pushing him back via blows with such an intensity that he continued walking backwards while defending himself. I was blinded mad by my anger while hitting him from all angles as he walked backwards for a good distance. Then he turned to my right and without realizing it, we both began walking and stumbling all over the sitting troops. The troops were the spectators screaming and clapping as if they were sitting at the New York Madison Square Garden attending a boxing match for the heavy weight champion of the world. We had passed the third road of sitting trainees on a one-sided furious engagement when my Staff Sergeant jumped in between us and grabbed me to prevent me from stick-punching my opponent anymore. I stopped, came back to my senses, and thanked my sergeant for intervening. He was laughing in a friendly way, hugged me and took me away from my opponent and from the group of soldiers still sitting on the ground, and he said, "You got the ass" uhm! He meant you got mad! It was quite an experience getting to know what one can do when provoked. In a moment of rage, to lose self-control and become a dangerous individual, and in the process, hurt someone without realizing it. My challenger was fine, thank God, and I felt sorry for what had happened and told others that that was not the real me. I thought about it and realized that one could hurt seriously another human being during those few minutes of uncontrollable ire. The weapons used as a training tools were designed in such a way that no one could get hurt. The rapid anger response also amps up your brain. It helps you quickly know a potential threat, which was what I felt. It can push you to make impulsive decisions in the heat of the moment. It's no surprise anger is linked to accidents and risky activities like smoking, gambling, drinking, and overeating.

While I was assigned to Fort Gordon, Georgia, I met a trainee that was a Cuban immigrant, last name Munoz, who had a college degree. In addition, he had been a Cuban Air Force pilot and had ascended to the rank of lieutenant and had to his record many hours of flying time and many parachute jumps. His Cuban rank of Lieutenant did not count here in the USA Army. However, he could rise in rank quicker than others because of his military experience and qualifications.

I was pleased to get along fine with him, and I used to look forward to his advice when I needed help. The two-month Advance Infantry training at Fort Gordon was ending. We were given three options for our next assignment; 1) allow the Army to choose for you your next assignment, 2) volunteer for a three-year extension to your two year tour of duty, and follow a non-commission officer Army career path and 3) volunteer to become a paratrooper by attending Paratrooper School at Fort Benning, Georgia, where training would be provided for three consecutive weeks until graduating as a paratrooper. Upon graduation as a paratrooper one would get an increase in monthly salary of $50.00 without any time extension on our tour of duty.

We were given a few days to think about our options. I met with Munoz to talk about our available options and he, without any hesitation, had already decided to volunteer to become a US paratrooper. He had jumped out of airplanes while in Cuba and felt that I could do it too. He also emphasized that there was no need to extend our time with the Army after the completion of the airborne training. Also, he said, I would get an additional $50 increase in my monthly salary. After some hesitation regarding the dangers of jumping out of airplanes; broken legs, arms, ribs, and the like, I went along with Munoz and signed up for airborne training. Munoz and I were transferred to Fort Benning, Georgia, to begin airborne training.

Jump training was considered the roughest, most intensive training in the Army. We all had to learn and practiced many times procedures which had to become mechanical in the split-second timing which in parachuting means the difference between safe landing into combat or death. The making of the paratrooper had been studied until it was developed into a science. The paratrooper had to be toughened physically and mentally to jump from airplanes unhesitatingly and to land ready for combat as may be needed.

The Army Days

Army Days: Basic Training at Fort Dix, NJ. And Advance
Infantry Training at Fort Gordon, GA

Chapter 18

Jump School

THERE WAS A DISTINGUISHING statement made with pride by those that had already earned their paratrooper wings that said, *paratroopers were not born, they were made*. The proper development of a paratrooper was the result of many studies that led to the best training techniques to the point that it was scientific. The established training procedures had to be followed to ensure that the paratrooper was tough physically and mentally conditioned, and ready to not only unwaveringly jump from airplanes but to land readily and safely to engage in battle with enemy soldiers.

The moment a volunteer started airborne training, the physical requirements get steadily more rugged and difficult. The mental development progresses slowly to increasingly difficult tests developed to permit only the best to get through. I was fortunate that I had always been of the athletic type that loves physical exercise. I had no problem getting used to the continuous physical demand exerted by the trainers which were referred to as "the Gorillas."

These trainers or gorillas were selected because of their experience and knowledge of airborne. The Gorillas were feared, hated, and admired at the same time due to their dedication to develop good airborne soldiers. When they talked, you listened; when they said, "give," you gave; when they said, "jump," you jumped. They were responsible for the development and training of the fit and for identifying the unfit.

There were many mock-ups built to provide familiarity with actual airplanes. These mock-ups included the harnesses structure to get you used to hanging from a parachute, rope climbing structures to simulate returning to the plane while in flight or sliding yourself down from a parachute that may have been caught up in a tree. The wind machine was used to learn to release yourself once you reached the ground and were faced with strong ground winds that blow your parachute and you away from a landing target.

Jump training was rough and intensive at the Army training facilities of Fort Benning. Paratroopers had to be able to react in a split-second which could be the difference between surviving and dying. Jump School was designed to develop that type of soldier. There were only two grades in Jump School; Superior and Failure. The jump Training Program consisted of three weeks; Ground, Tower, and Jump week.

Jump School is not open only to regular soldiers but to officers of any rank; Lieutenant, Captain, Major, General and other high-ranking officers. We were all mixed having the same rank in the eyes of training sergeants and everyone was referred to by an assigned number. I was number 645, and training sergeants addressed me as 645 rather than by my name. In a similar manner every high-ranking officer was addressed by their respective assigned numbers. A training sergeant could ask officers to drop and do many pushups or run many laps around the barracks, if he saw it appropriate.

The first week, referred to as the *Ground Week*, included many hours of physical training: trotting, learning, and practicing new exercises. We were not allowed to walk anywhere. If we had to go to the mess hall for our regular meals: breakfast, lunch, or dinner, we had to run or jog but never walked regardless of the time of the day. In case we were walking or jogging too slow and the Training Sargent saw us, we were penalized by having to perform many exercises (pushups or laps around the barracks) right on the spot while we were yelling loud and clear many times "I will not walk again, Sargent."

The ground week training program also ensured that before you get to jump out of an airplane you had first learned how to land on the ground safely. You had to practice until you learned to land, loaded with about 36 pounds of combat equipment, and 15 pounds of a reserve parachute plus your own weight, in my case about 180 pounds for a total 231 pounds.

For our safety we had to learn the skills required to transition from a descending condition to a safe landing by dissipating the energy upon hitting the ground over our entire body, preventing injury. We were taught how to wear the parachute harness correctly and how to use the special training gear. We spent many hours learning, practicing, and perfecting the parachute landing fall.

The idea was landing with your feet and knees together and bent while moving the upper part of your body sideways until reaching the ground, preventing that your legs and feet support the entire weight of your body causing injury to either legs or feet. It was very important to practice landing from a 3-foot high wood platform simulating arrival after jumping off the airplane exit. Again, as we approached the ground our knees had to be bent and loose to prevent injury. We had to fall sideways toward the right or left as we saw appropriate. I completed the ground week to the satisfaction of the training sergeants and moved on to the second week.

The second week was referred to as the *Tower Week*, you had to pass all landing training tests and the physical fitness requirements. Trainees that were unable to advance required additional training or were "recycled" to another class due to lack of progress or injury.

The focus of the second week of Jump School was jumping from two towers of different altitudes, a 34-foot and a 250-foot tower respectively. The 34-foot tower was used to simulate exiting an aircraft while in flight. We began using the 34-foot tower and the swing-landing trainer, the suspended harness, and later the 250-foot tower that simulated descending from a high altitude after exiting the aircraft in flight.

We became familiar with the mock-up door trainer to simulate mass exit from an aircraft in flight. We were taught the different phases of parachute flight from an aircraft exit, through the parachute opening shock, chute deployment, then onto the deployment of the risers, steering the chute, and all the way to landing. We began this second training week jumping out of the 34-foot tower. The 34-foot tower consisted of a 12 x 10-foot wooden room located on top of a 34-foot wooden structure which simulated an inflight aircraft, the trainees having to jump from exits located on each side of the elevated room.

The mock-up 34-foot tower was where more would-be troopers quit than in any other stage of the training program. This mock-up tower was built to about the height of a four-story window on a regular building. Looking down from this equivalent window was a terrifying experience to those of us that were not used to it. The ground below was packed as hard as concrete and, therefore, scary to many trainees including me.

The trainees wore a strong harness designed to simulate a real parachute harness. The harness was hung from a cable line inside the mock-up tower and trainees, upon the instructor's command, shuffled to the exits. The length of the cable starting at the 34-foot tower exit to the landing spot at ground level was about 150 feet. That is, the cable terminated at the point where another trainee was waiting for those that had the nerve to jump, to catch them and thereby provide a smooth landing upon their arrival.

At the start of the jump, that is, at the point of exit you were given the command "jump", and you would begin a free fall for about four seconds. After the four seconds free fall, the cable would pick up the slack and one would slide hanging from the cable or rope to the other end where someone was waiting for you. In my view, that was the hardest and scariest part of the training program, jumping out of that tower.

When it was my turn to climb the stairs to get up the four-story tower, my legs were trembling, my breathing was heavy and, in general I was shaky, moving toward the unknown, the unexpected, but thinking that since others were jumping, I could probably do the same. When it was my turn, and I was told "One man at the door" I shuffled to the exit as instructed and I froze there! I could not jump. I looked down the four-story height and "Oh God! What am I doing up here! I was not able to jump. The sergeant shouted "Jump! Soldier!" I said. I can't. "The sergeant shouts once again "Jump!" "I am trying sergeant, but I can't!" I said. Then he responded, "Then quit and go back down" "I am not quitting!" I said. He said. "I want you to scream loud and clear," "I am not a quitter, Sergeant." I did scream loud and clear "I am not a quitter, Sergeant!" I was holding up the line of trainee-jumpers waiting for me to clear the exit, either by jumping or quitting. I did not have the weakness to quit. The sergeant followed with a "Then jump soldier!" I said; "I can't jump, I need a push! Push me sergeant," I said again.

The sergeant asked me once again, "You are not quitting, are you?" "No, I am not!" Then he gave me a push via a gentle kick on my butt, and down I went onto a free fall for about four seconds, and as I was on a free fall for those four seconds, I screamed long and loud "Oh Shit! Oh Shit!". The rope with my body weight and the extra gear soon picked up the slack and I, hanging from the now taught rope, glided toward the end of the rope where I was caught by others. I was so proud of myself that within my inner self I was screaming "I did it! I did it!" What a moment that was for me. That was my first jump, there were many more jumps to come. I needed five qualified jumps to get a passing grade.

My first and subsequent jumps illustrated to others what not to do when jumping out of an airplane. When I jumped, my legs were wide open, and swinging back and forth, my arms were flapping up and down like trying to grab something that was not there, and my body took many indescribable positions. I was told that my body had to be straight, my hands holding the handles of the reserve parachute ready to activate it. My legs had to be straight and together with my knees and heals touching each other, and my knees slightly bend. Of course, that did not happen during my first and subsequent four jumps.

As the saying continued all over the training camp, that *paratroopers were not born, they were made.* In the evening after the intensive day-time training, I had to jog to the mess hall for dinner and back, running fast and eager to get into my bed.

There was another potential paratrooper whom I met at Fort Gordon, Georgia. He, just like me, volunteered for jump training and was transferred along with me to Fort Benning. I admired him because of his physique, bulging arm and leg muscles, well defined abdominal muscles and someone that appeared to have exercised all his life. He was heavier than I was but shorter by about two inches. He was also much younger, nice looking, a quiet but friendly soldier. He had completed the first week of training without any problem and moved on to the second week.

That evening, after returning from the day's training of Tower Week, he confided that he would be quitting the next day. "Why?" I asked. He replied almost in tears, "I can't jump out of that 34-foot tower. Today, as I was waiting for my turn to jump off the top of 34-foot tower, I started trembling with fear. I found out that I suffer from acrophobia." "What is that?" "I asked. I am afraid of heights," he said. He continued, "I turned around and told the Sargent I had to go to the bathroom". He allowed me to go but I knew that he suspected that I was afraid and said nothing.

My friend did resign the following morning. I learned that one can be tough physically but mentally weak or affected by other mental issues which was not the right combination to develop paratroopers. You could not be afraid of heights and you had to jump out of the 34-foot tower which led to jumping from airplanes unhesitatingly. It was a necessity for all paratroopers. I never saw my friend again.

When it was my turn to jump a second time, I was able to jump on my own, without being pushed by anyone. It was great that I was able to jump on my own, but I could not control my body movements, my arms, and leg positions. I jumped many times during the tower week and finally I failed the training week. My legs kept controlling my position. I did not give up. I was very motivated and determined to become a paratrooper. I had such a positive attitude and thought that failure was not an option. Those that failed the second week, the tower week, were given an additional opportunity to repeat it the following week. I repeated the week and was able to successfully perform the five qualified jumps needed and proceeded to complete the Tower Week.

The week ended with open parachute drops from a 250-foot high tower. That was another challenging activity, a second tower where you would be lifted and dropped from a height of 250 feet with a parachute wide open. That tower was used for the first descend by parachute, a 250-foot tower. The trainee did not climb the tower but was lifted by a cable and released after reaching the height of a 25-story building. Once we were pulled up to the tower top, we could get a good look at the local geography. The trainee, once he left the ground, felt helpless. There was no place to go but upward and then released downward. The trainees were released from either one of the three sides of the tower, the fourth side was not used depending on the direction of the wind to prevent the trainee from colliding against the steel tower. The selection of which sides to use was always a function of the wind direction at the time of jumping. A pulley machine will take the trainees to the top of the tower and then drop them whether they liked it or not. The first time I had no idea what to expect but after the first drop, the four subsequent drops became a routine activity.

The third week, the Jump Week was the last phase of the airborne training program. The future paratroopers would get to practice their new skills by jumping out of real aircraft in flight, the C-130 aircraft. The Air Force aircraft fly at 1200 feet above the ground at an airspeed of about 150 MPH. After the flight crew completed the pre-drop and slow-down checklists, trainees rose out of their seats and moved at the jump-master's direction to one of two paratroop doors located on each side of the aircraft.

Everyone was silent and not willing to express their fear and anxiety of jumping for the first time from an altitude of about 1250 foot. This altitude is the usual aircraft flying altitude that trainees could be dropped from the airplane. There was a Jump Master, who was an experienced jumper, responsible for the group, checking that everyone had their gear correctly attached to their bodies including a reserve chute carried by each in the front part of the body.

At the "green light" one group of trainees exited the plane, jumpers continued to shuffle to the door until the red light was illuminated. At that point the aircraft begun its racetrack maneuver circling back to the beginning of the drop zone and continued to do this until all jumpers had jumped. A soldier had to complete 5 jumps, including one-night jump, to graduate from Airborne School.

Any time we boarded the aircraft we felt anxiety. We looked at each other wondering about the imminent jump.

When you are seating against one of the side walls of the plane in a tight seating arrangement you look casually at the man seated at your right and at your left as well as to those seated across the aisle on the opposite wall across from you. You could hear the heavy breathing from those seated close to you and saw their sweat emanating and running down their foreheads as we were flying toward the drop zone. Not all the sweating was derived from the airplane's heat (it was summer, and the aircraft had no air-conditioning) but from everyone's extra perspiration. An hour and a half of flying time to the drop zone seemed an eternity, until eventually the plane reached the drop zone.

What I felt, and I am sure everyone else felt the same way too, was that our anxiety feelings began when we were told that we were scheduled to jump and had to be at the airport at a given time. We boarded the aircraft, usually a C-130 Cargo Plane, where we sat against the two aircraft walls in two rows facing each other. As we continued boarding, seating, and waiting for takeoff, we began feeling the *anxiety,* started *sweating* and became tense and eager to get out of that warm aircraft as soon as possible while praying that within the estimated four seconds that chute would open.

We had to be brave enough to stand up when the Jump Master said, "Get ready." We had to place the right foot forward getting ready to stand up. The next command was "Stand up" followed by 'One man left door" or "right door," depending on which side you were seated. Once the order to "Stand up", followed by "One-man left door" or

"One-man right door" was given, we started shuffling toward the door. We had to be careful and alert always. The Jump Master could say, "One-man front door," and since regular planes do not have front doors, we better not move upon the issuance of the incorrect command. Once each of us shuffled forward and stood at the door, the Jump Master gave the command "Go!" You would then jump away from that door for which we had been trained, without questioning or saying, "Why am I jumping?" You positioned yourself at the door with each hand holding each side of the of the open door waiting for the command "Go". When the command "Go" was given, we pushed ourselves away from that door, assumed our jumping position and began a free fall that lasted about four seconds. The free fall would stop after the initial slack on the rip cord became tight, the connecting lace freed the chute and the wind opened the chute. You were supposed to feel the pull of the rip cord, attached to the chute on your back. Within a maximum of four seconds it would open followed by hearing the loud and clear opening of that giant umbrella against the wind above your head, slowing you down after that initial free fall.

The chute opened, wide open, and we all looked back to the aircraft and saw it moving away from us. The chute looked so green, pretty, and one exclaimed; "Thank you Lord!" It opened as anticipated, but one was always concerned. The beauty and happiness emerged when we were descending. The day was very clear, the sky was blue, and we looked down toward the ground and admired the scenery. If it was not windy, we just concentrated on a safe landing. When we felt the hardness of the ground and verified that every part of our body was in shape, we exclaimed: "Mission accomplished!" Many screamed and cursed while others laughed, but the overall feeling was that of accomplishment. We had one additional jump to our records. We would jump without any hesitation. We looked at each other but nobody talked except when the Sergeant in charge questioned someone.

There were a few but rare instances when after the jumper had exited the aircraft, the jumper found himself on top of the open chute of the man who had just jumped in front of you. If that happened, it was our responsibility to walk over his chute and away from it as rapidly as you could to continue your own descent. It never happened to me but just thinking about it scared me.

We were supposed to make five jumps out of an airplane, land safely, and at the end of that week we had a graduation ceremony when our hard-earned paratrooper wings would be pinned upon our chests. I was trying to be indifferent and casual, but my chest raised arrogantly as the sought-after wings were pinned on my chest. I was now a paratrooper ready and eager to walk proudly in front of those that felt that I was not going to make it, to walk among those that were referred to as "legs" because they failed physically or were physically fit but mentally incapable of jumping. There were those with bulging, well defined muscles throughout their bodies but mentally unable to jump. The photographs on the following pages illustrate specific sequencial instances of anxiety, sweat, tension, bravery, relief and gladness that each paratrooper trainee felt prior to boarding the aircraft, during flight, after exiting the aircraft and eventualy landing on the ground safely.

LOUIS RODRIGUEZ

34- Foot Training Tower

Courtesy of my 1963 Year Book

250-Foot Training Tower

Airborne Training at Fort Benning, Georgia. Jumping from
a 250 Feet Tower

Courtesy of my 1963 Year Book

Jumping Off C130 Aircraft

Troopers in Training Jumping from C130 Aircraft Flying at an Altitude of 4000 Feet Prior to Graduation as a Paratrooper. Courtesy of 1962 Paratrooper Jump School book

Other Moments of Army Days

Wearing; Parachute, Reserve Chute, and Class A Uniform
and my Paratrooper Wings proudly.

Chapter 19

101st Airborne Division

AFTER MY GRADUATION from Jump School, I was given transfer orders to the 101st Airborne Division located at Fort Campbell, Kentucky. Fort Campbell was a United States Army installation located across the Kentucky-Tennessee border between Hopkinsville, Kentucky, and Clarksville, Tennessee.

Fort Campbell was home to the 101st Airborne Division and the 160th Special Operations Aviation Regiment. The 101st Airborne Division was a division of the United States Army trained for air assault operations. The 101st Airborne Division was nicknamed the "Screaming Eagles" for their division insignia, an eagle. During World War II, it was renowned for its role in Operation Overlord (the D-Day landings and airborne landings on June 6, 1944, in Normandy, France), Operation Market Garden, the liberation of the Netherlands and, perhaps most famously, its action during the Battle of the Bulge around the city of Bastogne, Belgium. The division's primary method of delivering troops into combat was the use of airplanes. Division headquarters was at Fort Campbell, Kentucky. The division is one of the most highly decorated units in the United States Army and has been featured prominently in military fiction. Fort Campbell was to be my permanent post for the remainder of the two-year draft, about 18 months. The Division consisted of many companies including a Head Quarters Unit. I was assigned to Company E of the 501st Airborne Division. Then I was transferred to Headquarters, 1st Airborne Battle Group where I was trained as a radar operator for the remaining Army duty time.

Once assigned to my permanent post, I could ask Lylia to fly from NYC to Nashville airport since I was now permitted to live off post. I found a small apartment in the city of Clarksville, on the Tennessee side. I rented the apartment which was located on a second floor of a two-family home owned by Mrs. McCorkle. Lylia and I could live together as the Army expected us to do. I went via bus to pick her up at the Nashville Airport. I could not believe her appearance when I saw her. She was oversized. I had not seen her for approximately four months, and I was expecting a skinny but well-shaped lady and, Wow! She was now about seven months pregnant. I was happy, and I admired the beauty of nature and of what she was carrying inside, a beautiful baby, either a son or daughter, made no difference. A blessing was on its way to this earth which would make us happy upon his or her arrival.

We took a bus from Nashville back to the city of Clarksville and to the apartment I had just rented at the home of Mrs. McCorkle. I commuted by hitch hiking daily to Fort Campbell to fulfill my army responsibilities. Once I felt that Lylia and I were settled at one place for a relative long period of time, about 18 months, I started looking for a night school to begin improving my education, hoping to get a better job after the army days were over.

I found later that the Army would not allow me to drive an army vehicle because the results of the battery of tests I had taken on many subjects at the New York Induction Center showed that my Intelligence Quotient (IQ) score, a score determined by one's performance on a standardized intelligence test relative to the average performance of others of the same age, indicated that I was a moron! Others in my platoon did not think so since during my spare time I used to play chess and I very seldom lost a game even among the stronger players. Many in my platoon and at the Service Club considered me a strong chess player who was very difficult to defeat. I felt that the results of the IQ test illustrated my lack of education combined with my lack of reading, writing, speaking, and understanding English at the time I took the test.

I obtained my State of Tennessee driver's license without any problem. I bought a second-hand car, a Dodge Swept-Wing, 1957, for my daily transportation between Clarksville and Fort Campbell. I thought that it was a nice-looking old car, but I had no idea how bad it was inside. The car worked fine for a few weeks until I started spending money on repairs. The car almost killed me when I left it at the repair shop one morning for an oil change. I returned in the afternoon to pick it up, and the car was still up on the lift. I decided to look underneath the trunk, specifically in the area where the shock absorbers were located. I moved cautiously toward the back springs without touching anything. The next thing I know is the shock absorber closest to me snapped in two halves because of old age, and one of the halves of the back spring swung in a clockwise direction in a pendulum fashion in front of my face with such speed and force but without touching me. I said, "The Lord was protecting me." The two halves were still swinging back and forth when the auto shop owner rushed toward the back of the lift to ask me if everything was ok. Thank God, it was.

Two months had gone by when my entire platoon was scheduled to perform regular field training duties. On this day we were learning how to exit out of a helicopter while in flight and using a rope to slide down to the ground. It was an interesting and exciting training activity and while on training a young Army Lieutenant was looking for me to tell me that I had to go home because my wife was very sick, and I had to bring her to the army hospital right away. I drove home which was about half hour ride from Fort Campbell and found her having miscellaneous painful cramps. She told me that the baby was due to arrive, and it was time for me to take her to the hospital, which I did. On September 25, 1962, a lovely daughter was born at the hospital facilities of Fort Campbell, Kentucky. We had to give her a name before leaving the hospital. We named our daughter Alice Mabel Rodriguez. It turned out that in later years she was not too happy with her middle name, Mabel. We were not prepared for her arrival and, therefore, we removed one drawer from a four-drawer wooden-chest and used it as a baby crib. Lylia used blankets placed at the bottom of the drawer as mattress, and other clothes as pillows to make the baby comfortable.

We had now a family of three members, and when time allowed it, we used to go to the neighboring park carrying blankets, a basket with food and sodas and we had a picnic. The photographs that follow illustrate the family days while on army duty at Fort Campbell, Ky.

Family Life a Fort Campbell Ky

Earned My Paratrooper Wings, Welcomed to Fort
Campbell, KY and Living Off Post with my Family in
Clarksville, Tennessee. Courtesy my family album.

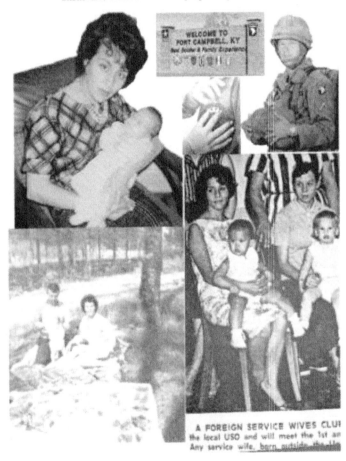

A FOREIGN SERVICE WIVES CLUB
the local USO and will meet the 1st an
Any service wife, born outside the U.S.

Chapter 20

Cuban Crisis

MY RESPONSIBILITIES while in the army were usually related to performing routine warfare field-practices in preparation for a potential Battle Group deployment to resolve a crisis. I belonged to 1st Airborne Battle Group, 501st Infantry of the 101st Airborne Division, which was a combat ready unit, ready to go anywhere in the world as warranted by the specific crisis.

This ready status was referred as an "Alert status" which was a rotating 24-hours a day duty with other battle groups throughout the Division. This meant that the Battle Group could be called to perform war duty activities within a few days after the issuance of official orders by Washington. Therefore, my duties, in addition to be a regular paratrooper, included being ready to jump anywhere in the world loaded with a duffel bag, an M15-automatic rifle, hand-grenades, canteen, bayonet and other miscellaneous equipment. I was also responsible for the use of radar equipment. The radar was used to detect footsteps of the enemy during night training sessions simulating combat duty. The radar equipment was not sophisticated, it was easy to use, and I had to be ready to use it whenever the appropriate time arrived.

My paratrooper activities became a daily routine where I would do either kitchen police (KP), guard duty, cleaning the barracks, working with others cleaning the open-type army toilets and showers area or performing physical exercises during early mornings to stay in shape. In addition, we were required to jump out of an aircraft as called for by a Jump Schedule.

That routine was broken in October 1962, after being a 101st Airborne Division paratrooper for about three months. The relations between the United States and Cuba, the Caribbean island, had been deteriorating since Fidel Castro seized power in early 1959, and President Dwight D. Eisenhower closed the American embassy in Havana and severed diplomatic relations.

That action indicated that the United States was prepared to take extreme measures to oppose Castro's regime. The U.S. officials were worried that Cuba would become a strategic position of communism in the western hemisphere. The immediate reason cited for the break was Castro's demand that the U.S. embassy staff be reduced, which followed heated accusations from the Cuban government that America was using the embassy as a base for spies.

Severing relations with Cuba marked the end of America's policy of trying to resolve its differences with Castro's government through diplomacy. Just over two months later, President John F. Kennedy unleashed the Cuban exile-force established during the Eisenhower years. This led to the Bay of Pigs disaster, which began in

April 17, 1961 when a CIA-financed, armed-trained group of about 1500 Cuban refugees landed in the Bahía de Cochinos (Bay of Pigs) on the south coast of Cuba in an attempt to topple the communist government of Fidel Castro. The attack was a complete failure, Castro's military killed or captured the exile troops. After the Bay of Pigs, the relationship between the United States and Cuba was the most hostile of the Cold War.

In October 1962, the Cuban Missile Crisis was the result of the United States direct and dangerous confrontation with the Soviet Union during the Cold War. It was a moment when the two world powers came very close to a nuclear conflict. Construction of several missile sites began in the late summer, but U.S. intelligence discovered evidence of a general Soviet arms build-up on Cuba, which included Soviet IL–28 bombers.

On September 4, 1962, President Kennedy issued a public warning against the introduction of offensive weapons into Cuba. Despite the warning, on October 14 a U.S. U–2 aircraft took several pictures clearly showing sites for medium-range and intermediate-range ballistic nuclear missiles (MRBMs and IRBMs) under construction in Cuba. These images were processed and presented to the White House the next day, thus precipitating the start of the Cuban Missile Crisis.

The White House and the Kremlin were discussing a solution to the crisis with relatively little input from the respective bureaucracies typically involved in the foreign policy process. The essential point was that the Russians began transporting missiles via ships that were scheduled for arrival in Cuba.

President Kennedy summoned his closest advisers to consider options and direct a course of action for the United States that would resolve the crisis. Some advisers (including all the Joint Chiefs of Staff) argued for an air strike to destroy the missiles, followed by a U.S. invasion of Cuba; others favored stern warnings to Cuba and the Soviet Union. The President decided upon a middle course. On October 22, he ordered a naval "quarantine" of Cuba. The use of "quarantine" legally distinguished this action from a blockade, which assumed a state of war existed; the use of "quarantine" instead of "blockade" also enabled the Unites States to receive the support of the Organization of American States.

On October 24, Khrushchev responded to Kennedy's message with a statement that the U.S. "blockade" was an "act of aggression" and that Soviet ships bound for Cuba would be ordered to proceed. Nevertheless, during October 24 and 25, some ships turned back from the quarantine line; others were stopped by U.S. naval forces, but they contained no offensive weapons and could proceed. Meanwhile, U.S. reconnaissance flights over Cuba indicated the Soviet missile sites were nearing operational readiness. With no apparent end to the crisis in sight, U.S. forces were placed on Alert, meaning that war involving the Strategic Air Command was imminent.

On October 26, Kennedy told his advisors it appeared that only a U.S. attack on Cuba would remove the missiles, but he insisted on giving the diplomatic channel more time. The crisis had reached a virtual stalemate. Although U.S. experts were convinced the message from Khrushchev was authentic, hope for a resolution was short-lived.

In the evening of October 26, Khrushchev sent Kennedy a long, emotional message that raised the threat of nuclear holocaust, and presented a proposed resolution. "If there is no intention," he said, "to doom the world to the catastrophe of thermonuclear war, then let us not only relax the forces pulling on the ends of the rope, let us take measures to untie that knot. We are ready for this."

The next day, October 27, Khrushchev sent another message indicating that any proposed deal must include the removal of U.S. Jupiter missiles from Turkey. That same day, a U.S. U–2 reconnaissance jet was shot down over Cuba. Kennedy and his advisors prepared for an attack on Cuba within days as they searched for any remaining diplomatic resolution.

It was determined that Kennedy would ignore the second Khrushchev message and respond to the first one. That night, Kennedy set forth in his message to the Soviet leader proposed steps for the removal of Soviet missiles from Cuba under supervision of the United Nations, and a guarantee that the United States would not attack Cuba.

In October 1962, Company E 501st Infantry of the 101st Airborne Division, my battle group, was given orders to prepare for an assault on Cuba. We were all very concerned with the reality of what was about to take place. We were usually kept in the dark as to any specific plans that had already been approved for implementation by the upper echelon. We were not supposed to ask questions just follow orders. Those of us that were living off post were given instructions to advise our wives of the imminent departure for Cuba. The paratroopers' salaries were paid in advance of our regular payment date with instructions to give them to our respective families and to explain that we had no idea when we would be returning home. I drove home to Clarksville and dropped the check, got a few sets of clean clothes, and hugged my wife and my little daughter, and explained that I had no idea of a return date and gave her instructions to pray for our safe return.

I drove back to Fort Campbell where there was a serious commotion everywhere related to the potential assault on Cuba and possible war with the Soviet Union. We were issued weapons and ammunition, an action that was rare because we usually were issued weapons without ammunition. The rumor among us was that the battle groups of the 101st Airborne Division would be the first to jump into Cuba at a key location. The speculation was unimaginable, and panic was everywhere, and we were not even aboard the aircrafts yet. The C130 aircrafts were ready to be loaded with paratroopers upon the issuance of orders to fly over Cuba. Comments included: "The number of casualties from our battle group would be extremely high", that "by the time we landed in Cuba we all would be dead or nearly dead", that "the Cubans would be using our airborne parachutes and bodies for target practice", and "let us make sure that "we say goodbye to each other because the end is near."

As reported by our sergeant in charge, the Cuban Missile crisis, a direct and dangerous confrontation between the United States and the Soviet Union, came the closest to a nuclear conflict as ever before. It ended October 28, 1962, when the Soviet Leader agreed to remove the missiles from Cuba in an exchange for a promise from the United States to respect the sovereignty of Cuba's territory.

I, like many other members of the 101st Airborne Division, was delighted to hear the good news. Cheers were heard everywhere, and phone calls were made to our families to share the great news that we were not going anywhere on that unforgeable October 1962. My little daughter Alice was barely a month old. I continued attending my night school to improve my education.

Chapter 21

New York City

I WAS ATTENDING night school diligently in preparation to take the General Educational Development (GED) examination while still performing my army duties. General Educational Development (GED) was a group of five subject tests which, when passed, certified that the test taker had American high school-level academic skills. Although the "GED" acronym is frequently mistaken as meaning "general education degree" or "general education diploma", the American Council on Education, which owns the GED trademark, coined the acronym to identify "tests of general educational development." These tests measure proficiency in science, mathematics, social studies, reading, and writing. Passing the GED test gives those who do not complete high school, or who do not meet requirements for a high school diploma, the opportunity to earn their high school equivalency credential in the majority of the United States.

At that time, the test had to be taken in person and in the presence of a representative from the American Council on Education. The State and corresponding jurisdictions awarded a Certificate of High School Equivalency or similarly titled credential to persons who met the passing score requirements. The test was also given on military bases in more traditional settings. The army had authorized institutions to teach the five main subjects. I attended night school to prepare for taking the GED examination. I felt that with my adulthood experiences, my commitment and motivation, I should be able to pass the tests and get my GED diploma. I was very proud that slowly I was getting myself educated. Saturdays and Sundays were study days for me and also nights whenever possible, that is, when I was not performing my regular army duties. Upon completion of miscellaneous GED courses, I took the examination and passed successfully.

In mid-1963, while still at Fort Campbell, KY for the remaining of my 2-year tour of duty, I began counting the days left for my discharge from my Army duty, I was eager for time to go by fast and to become a short-timer as they referred to those that had a few months left in the Army. I was looking forward to an Honorable Discharged from the 101st Airborne Division.

I appreciated the time I spent as a member of the US armed forces, starting with the Induction Center in NYC and moving on to Fort Dix, New Jersey, Fort Gordon, Georgia, Fort Benning, Georgia and to Fort Campbell, Kentucky, my final destination for the remaining of my tour of duty. I learned at every Fort to be disciplined, obey orders, be punctual, army boots "spit shined", footlocker organized, and uniforms starched. I was told by my sergeant many times that if I had one button of my shirt or my pants unbuttoned, all the buttons were unbuttoned, and I was to be punished for it.

My platoon sergeant shouted at me during an inspection procedure, "Soldier", he said. "Yes Sergeant," I replied. He continued, "Your shirt sleeves are too short! Did you hear me! Too short!" I replied, "No sergeant. "What happens is that my arms are too long!" The sergeant became furious and started screaming at me, "You think I am stupid? Your sleeves are too short! I don't want to see you with that shirt again and you better drop and give me 25 pushups!" That was how one became an organized and a disciplined soldier who made sure shirts and pants fit properly.

After the completion of my military service, I was honorably discharged in February 1964. It was time to return to NYC. I had no idea what was in store for me in NYC, but I was eager to return. Two years in the USA Army had been great and enough for me. I was better prepared to undertake whatever would be coming my way. I improved my ability to speak English and to understand when spoken to, although my writing skills were weak. I became organized and disciplined and most important I had taken the initial step to get an education. I had obtained a GED.

The 60s for me were like stepping into a time machine that transported me almost instantaneously from Colombia into an advanced world. I had moved to NYC; I was drafted into the United States armed forces and I was going back to NYC. My honorable discharge from the 101st Airborne Division was mailed to me sometime in April 1964.

My wife Lylia, our daughter, Alice, and I had slowly been preparing for my travel back to NYC. I packed my old car with our few belongings and started driving back from Clarksville, Tennessee to NYC. The trip was uneventful. We drove and drove, making short stops along the way for resting or eating something until we arrived at NYC. The '57 Dodge behaved nicely until I noticed a lamp on the dashboard that indicated oil needed. I stopped at the first gas station we found, and had the oil checked. The attendant told me "You don't have any oil. You could have burnt the engine." Wow! We were lucky! The man filled the oil chamber and we continued our way to NYC.

Noemi and her husband, Teofilo, were friends made prior to my entering the army. We asked them if we were able to stay at their place for a few days until we settled in our own place. They agreed, and we drove to their home. We stayed with them until we were able to get a permanent place that we could afford. I had a significant number of belongings that I could not take with me to the army: my suitcases, my clothes, a guitar, silverware, my tailor-made suits and coat, and other minor items. We tried to get our belongings back, but we were told that they had disappeared, and they had no idea what happened.

I went to the company where I used to work prior to my joining the army to get my old job back. The Manager told me that they had no openings at the time. I argued that his company had the responsibility to give me back my old job as per the USA government regulations, and he said that he was sorry, but he could not hire me back because there were no openings at the time. However, as we continued discussing my possibility of working for them again, I kept the conversation friendly, I explained that I had obtained my GED and that I was now better prepared to serve the company. He said something which I heard for the first time, "You are still young. Why not keep on studying by attending a Community College such as the NYC Community College?" I thought about it after leaving his office, and it made sense. I started looking for the NYC Community College and I found it and shortly thereafter I was applying for registration and hoping that I would be accepted. I was accepted and began studying during the evenings. I was happy and motivated about taking a second step in getting educated.

I recalled the statement made by a great leader, John F Kennedy, "Ask not what your country can do for you. Ask what you can do for your country." I applied that statement in a different way, "Ask not what others can do for me. Ask what I can do for myself." I began applying that rule continuously. The '60s were the time period for great musicians like the Beatles, the Van Dyke television show, Broadway shows, baseball leagues, color TV, the Cuban Crisis, Vietnam War, race discrimination, the rise of a great black leader, Martin Luther King, and his great speech "I have a dream", the hippies, famous movie actors like Clint Eastwood and Paul Newman, Marilyn Monroe and Muhammad Ali, the underdog that defeated the then world boxing champion Sony Liston.

In the '60s we also had very unhappy days such as on November 22, 1963, while I was still an army soldier, when President Kennedy was assassinated in Dallas, Texas. He was shot twice and an hour later Lee Harvey Wallace was arrested for the crime. On April 4, 1968, the civil rights leader Dr. Martin Luther King Jr. was assassinated. He was shot in Memphis, Tennessee. Then US Senator Robert F. Kennedy, (Bobby), was also assassinated in June 5, 1968.

I became an armed forces veteran with the right to get financial support from the USA government to continue my education. I had to maintain a minimum grade on any college courses taken toward a degree. Congress had recently, by unanimous vote of the House and Senate, enacted a bill providing a permanent program of "readjustment" benefits for those who became veterans of military service after Jan. 31, 1955. I was honorably discharged from the armed forces in February 1964. The new "Cold War GI Bill" offered education grants, housing loans and other "readjustment" assistance to persons who had served in active duty in the armed forces. The most important feature of the legislation, however, was its permanence and Congress' decision that veterans of service during the relative peace of the "cold war" were as entitled to readjustment assistance as those who served during World War II and the Korean War.

I applied for the GI Bill benefit a few months after beginning classes at the NY City Community College.

After receiving government approval, I began to submit my grades to the corresponding Government Agency for review and approval as I completed courses each semester. Once the grades were verified, the government mailed me a check for an amount enough to cover my books and related expenses. Because I was not able to get my old job back, I started searching for a job. Daniel, to whom I sold my 1957 Ford (my first car) prior to my departure for army duty, told me that based on my radar experience he could try to get me a job at his company. A few days went by and Daniel told me that he had arranged for an interview with someone from his company. I went to the interview and after the end of that interview I was offered a job. I accepted it without any hesitation, I was happy that I would now have a salary to support my family. I started working for Sterling Corporation, a company located in Brooklyn, NY, as an inspector of quality control and tester of electrical characteristics of the manufactured products.

I reported to Daniel, who was the Supervisor of the Quality Control and Electrical Testing Department. I received "on-the-job" training for a few weeks. I simultaneously started going to the NYC Community College at night. It was not difficult for me to learn the testing and quality control procedures to carry out my responsibilities. Daniel told me that casual dress would be the appropriate working dress code.

The company manufactured miscellaneous electrical and electronic components and small power transformers that were used in miscellaneous defense projects by the USA government. The department had the responsibility to ensure that company products were manufactured in accordance with engineered and designed specifications developed by the Engineering Department and approved for production by USA government inspectors. The individual components workmanship quality and electrical performance had to meet the highest standards during the performance of inspection procedures.

The company was small and most of the employees worked on the manufacturing of the individual components. There were employees operating transformer winding machines, insulating wired coils, ladies connecting leads to the start and finish of wires emanating from the wound transformer coils, men working on encapsulating the finished products, others managing the oven used to bake the epoxy resin and others dedicated to painting black or brown on the final products. Our Department had initial, intermediate, and final inspection tables with instruments that were used to measure the electrical characteristics of the products produced, primarily transformers of different sizes; small, medium, and large. I had to measure the core loss, and exciting current and detect insulation breakdowns utilizing amp meters, volt meters, insulation resistance ohmmeters and mega meters and other testing equipment. The department after completion of the quality and electrical inspection, accepted or rejected the failed components. The failed components were returned to the production department for corrective actions and the accepted components were packed in cardboard boxes and shipped to the client. It was a great learning experience working for this company. I liked the job. I felt that I was doing something important. It was a cleaned environment and I worked only eight hours per day' Every day there was a different technical problem to be solved. I arrived at 8:00 a.m. and left at 5:00 p.m. I was pleased with my job combined with my attendance at NYC Community College. I was taking as many credits as I could fit in my evening schedule because I was in a hurry to get educated. My job was the equivalent of working at a laboratory that complemented my Community College school work. At school, I learned the electrical circuit's theory and at work I had the opportunity to put in practice with actual components what I was learning at school. I studied elements such as current flow, voltage drops or rise, resonance circuits, resistance, reactance and impedance networks, AC and DC motors and other electrical theory subjects. I considered myself fortunate in having such an important arrangement.

Commuting was inconvenient at times especially getting out of work and taking various NY City Transit system trains to go to school, then back home, next morning back to work and then to school again, but I got used to the daily routine. I used to get home almost by midnight every school night. However, the traveling time was not wasted since I used it to read my college books. Lylia was supportive of my effort to get ahead. I spent nights attending school and weekends working on homework assignments or getting ready for quizzes. I regret that I could not have spent more time with my daughter and Lylia during the week and weekends due to the little available free time I had with only a few hour hours for sleeping. When I managed to get free time on weekends, we usually went to neighborhood parks or to Central Park in Manhattan. When we did go out my books went along with me to study for the next quiz or exam coming up the following week while Lylia and my little daughter Alice enjoyed being out.

At the NY City Community College, I had chosen electrical technology as my college major or specialization field. As time went on, I began taking more advanced math and liberal arts courses as prerequisites to start taking the electrical technology courses leading to an Associate in Applied Science (AAS) degree.

I was becoming more effective at performing my duties at Sterling Corporation. One year had gone by when I found out that I had to pay taxes to the IRS. I had to find someone that could help me complete the necessary forms. I did, and I fulfilled my obligation to the government.

The General Manager of Sterling was replaced with a new manager named Arthur. Daniel had a changing personality that at times annoyed others including me, but he was my boss and I made every effort to support him and to get along well with him. The new General Manager, Arthur, after a few months on the job was not getting along well with Daniel. Daniel was arrogant and obnoxious at times, believing that as a Supervisor of the Quality Control

Department he could get away with that behavior. Daniel bossed Arthur around and Arthur was obviously not happy about it. Arthur, the General Manager, approached me one morning toward the end of November 1965. He asked me if I was interested in becoming a Department Supervisor. I thought about it and felt that he wanted to get rid of Daniel. Then I thought that if I had said something in favor of supporting Daniel, Arthur was going to bring someone else to replace him. Based on that, I responded to Arthur; "Yes, I can handle it, no problem." My salary was increased, and Daniel was permanently laid off, sadly on the morning of December 24 of that year. I felt very sad for Daniel, but it was not my fault. It was not a great Christmas for Daniel's family while on the contrary my family was very pleased with my promotion and higher salary. Daniel could not blame anybody but himself for his behavior and I could not blame myself for what had happened. I took over the supervisor position and had a staff of about six qualified technicians.

Chapter 22

Department Supervisor

IT WAS SUCH A GOOD FEELING to become the Department Supervisor, the boss, the chief, with responsibility for the Quality Control and Electrical Testing of all the items manufactured by the Corporation. Despite my new position and higher salary, I continued attending night college classes. I was motivated to not give up studying but rather to look forward to one day getting an Associate in Applied Science (AAS) degree. My expected date to achieve this goal was toward the end of 1967.

I continued carrying out the scope of work of my supervisory position successfully. I became well known by almost all employees as someone who cooperated with the production department when called upon to resolve issues affecting the quality of the product. I considered myself a good leader. Almost a year had gone by when I was asked by the Chief Engineer, an electrical engineer named David Lieberman, who was responsible for the Engineering Department, to meet him at his office. I was asked if I would be interested in transferring to the engineering department to assist them in the design of transformers. I was so proud of just the fact that they were asking the question. I was somewhat worried about my ability to get the job done to their expectations. Was I ready? I don't know. However, I was going to be trained on the specifics of the designing of the various components and perhaps I should not worry about it. I was also taking critical and related technical courses at the Community College.

It was an offer I could not refuse. I said, "Yes, I would love to be part of your group and I do appreciate your thinking of me as your first choice for the position." I was officially transferred to the engineering offices and began on-the-job-training right away.

It was an interesting job with a very detail-oriented scope of work. The basic math that I was learning at night was needed along with a conceptual view of the final product. We had to develop detailed and flawless design drawings for the production shop to build from such drawings. If you made a design error, an entire production could go down the drain along with increase in production costs, staff down time and project delivery delays. I had someone looking over my shoulder, guiding me as needed to ensure that a high-quality design specification was developed. I learned slowly but surely the process and eventually was becoming proficient.

Despite that it was a very interesting job, way down deep in my mind was my original dream of traveling the world. My dream did not include sitting all day working in front of a desk with a hand calculator and pencil designing miscellaneous components and waiting for the bell to ring, so I could go to lunch or to my evening classes. Again, I had no idea how I would accomplish such a feat. I was patient yet determined to keep that dream alive. I believed that I was not ready to go anywhere yet. I continued working and taking as many electrical courses as I could handle at night toward my AAS degree. Time was flying, one semester after another toward my short-term objective, getting a college degree. Sterling's engineering department consisted of a chief engineer, one engineer and an assistant design engineer. When I looked around, I thought about the many years that the Chief Engineer and the engineer had been working for this company and I could not see myself in that small engineering department forever.

It did not take me long to think about moving on in search of a new and better job. I learned the basics of preparing a resume. I was beginning to have some work experience along with some college background that could be included in a resume. I developed a resume which emphasized the experience as an electrical tester, promoted to department supervisor and later to assistant design engineer at Sterling Corporation. I also mentioned my armed forces two-year duty with an honorable discharge. I had already taken some related courses which I could now add to my educational background and include in my first resume.

I started floating my resume and reading the newspapers' classified ads in search of a job with higher potential. My objective was to work for an engineering company that could use my recent qualifications and experience in the electrical field. I mailed my resume to a few companies including a company that provided electric power to commercial, industrial, and residential customers. This company, American Electric Power (AEP), had its headquarters in downtown Manhattan. AEP at the time was one of the largest electric utilities in the U.S., serving nearly three million customers in about 11 states. The company owned an electricity transmission lines network consisting of thousands of miles, at the time the largest in the nation with more 765-kilovolt of extra-high voltage transmission lines than many other U.S. transmission systems combined and large amounts of generating capacity in terms of megawatts. I thought that company could be good to work for.

The company, after reviewing my resume, asked me to go in for a series of interviews. I was very excited, of course! I reported to the company's offices in downtown Manhattan as scheduled. I was interviewed by various departments where the human resources felt they could use me. Human Resources also described for me the employee benefits: health insurance, vacations, and a savings plan. Human Resources also mentioned who would be interviewing me. Representatives from the following departments were scheduled to interview me: System Planning, Engineering and Design, Power Generation and Load and Energy Forecasting. The series of consecutive interviews lasted two days. Engineers and department heads spoke to me and asked me many questions. At the end of the second day I had to go back to the Human Resources department where I was told "Thank you for coming and we will let you know within about ten days the results of the interviews." I was hoping to hear from them on the spot but that was not the procedure and I had to wait. I did not have the slightest idea of the possible interviews' outcome, but I was hopeful for a positive answer. I was brought to various offices located on different floors to meet the engineers and department heads scheduled to interview me. I was thinking about what had transpired during the interviews. AEP employed hundreds of engineers of various disciplines at this building that occupied many floors. I was impressed with the number of engineers I saw working. I remembered the size of where I used to sit at Sterling, where the entire Engineering Department fit into two offices, one office dedicated to the Chief Engineer and the second office, I shared with one engineer.

The letter from AEP arrived a few days later with good news. I was made an offer to work for the AEP Transmission System Planning Section of the Regional Power Supply Planning Division at a specified annual salary. The salary was about 20 percent more than what I was making at Sterling Corporation. I was to report to work two weeks later after receipt of the appointment letter. That allowed me enough time to give Sterling a one-week notice advising them that I was leaving Sterling to work for AEP. The one week's notice went by and on the last day, after saying goodbye to everyone, I gathered my belongings and I was on my way to my new job. There was no farewell lunch or dinner or wishes for success as I learned it was customary with other companies.

Chapter 23

Engineering Technician

IT WAS MID 1967 when I reported to work to AEP wearing a suit and tie as my new dress code. I was there on time and ready to begin a new phase in my professional career. I was told during the interviews with the AEP Engineering staff that the company appreciated and welcomed those that were trying to better themselves through night school.

The AEP facilities were in downtown Manhattan in a tall building, very tall building by my Colombian perception for tall buildings. A Human Resources Department representative led me to what I thought was an impressive office located on the 11th floor. My desk was located on the left-hand side corner of the office as you walked into the room. It had a telephone, my own personal phone! I was told that my title would be Engineering Technician and that upon my graduation from college that title would be changed to Engineer. I was introduced to Charlie Falcone and Bengt Solomonson, two engineers I would be reporting to. Their desks were located on opposite corners of the square-shaped office near windows that had views to the outside. In the fourth corner of the office there was the desk of the Engineering Clerk. I was also going to have the help of an Engineering Clerk that reported to the two engineers and to me. I was fascinated by the soft red carpet that covered the office floor and the rest of the eleventh floor where our office was located. I was pleased, very pleased, and eager to start learning the scope of my work. It was around the summertime when I started my job at AEP.

The building was not too far from my new subway station in Battery Park. I started becoming familiar with the outside surroundings by wandering around the area near the building during my lunch hour. Battery Park was located within walking distance from my new office at AEP. The southern shoreline of Manhattan Island had long been known as "The Battery" since the 17th century when the area was part of the Dutch Settlement of New Amsterdam. The name Battery Park was most probably derived from an artillery battery that was located there at that time to protect the town from potential enemies coming from the sea. The Battery continued its function during the colonial era and was the center of Evacuation Day celebrations commemorating the departure of the last British troops from the United States after the American Revolutionary War.

I usually brought my lunch and walked over to the park where an empty public seating bench was always available. I felt that I was on the top of the world, at least for a few minutes a day. Many tourists from almost every state of the Union and from many other countries around the world came to visit Battery Park. It was just a great feeling sitting on that bench, just me, my thoughts, my sandwich, my soda, the view of the immensity of the Atlantic Ocean, the impressive view of the not too distant Statue of Liberty prominently rising on the horizon atop of Liberty Island. I thanked the Lord for allowing me to be there. It was just great, just me, sitting on that bench, and thinking that this is the top the world.

The main attraction of Battery Park was the dominant view of the Statue of Liberty and what it symbolized. The Statue of Liberty represented many things, including friendship between nations and freedom from oppression for its citizens. Prior to air traveling, ships would sail into the New York Harbor and the Statue of Liberty would welcome their passengers. Some were immigrants traveling to the United States for the first time, just like me when I came a few years earlier, except that I arrived at this great nation via airplane. The Statue of Liberty was then, and is today, one of the first sites seen when sailing into the harbor. The Statue was and continues to be a symbol of freedom.

I used to walk back to the office after finishing my lunch, take the elevator to the eleventh floor, and sit down to work. I thought that I had come a long way when I compared my new job to my first job at the toy company, Brillium Corporation. There was no more "toilet cleaning duty" or sweeping the floor of an entire toy company. I was moving forward one step at the time.

I began learning my responsibilities as an Engineering Technician of the Transmission System Planning Section while I continued attending night school at the community college. I was also getting older and at times I had to put up with jokes made by others behind my back which I happened to overhear. Charlie and Bengt, the two engineers I reported to, occasionally talked about my age with others and laughed about it. The jokes were related to the fact that their Engineering Technician was older than they were, not by much but it was true. I did not mind that at all. I felt that their comments were nothing compared with what I could learn from them as time went on. Their comments about me were insignificant compared with the reality that I was working with young but already industry recognized electrical engineers. Bengt held a master's degree in electrical engineering and Charlie was a holder of a Master and a PHD degree in electrical engineering. They were both graduates from prestigious engineering Universities. I was proud of being there and humble enough to understand how far down on the education ladder I was. I knew that I had a long way to go in my education. I listened in silence, without complaining, but with a resolution to continue in my night schooling. I acknowledged that it was rather late for many students to be going to school at my age, but I ignored any negative comments they or anybody made.

I was very pleased working for AEP. My department, the Transmission System Planning Department, was responsible for the development of short- and long-range transmission system plans designed to determine the best system configuration to deliver electrical power to small and large cities with many industrial, commercial, and residential customers served by AEP.

The analyses were performed using computer programs designed to study many alternative options. The alternatives were ranked from a technical viewpoint and the results of economic and financial evaluations leading to an optimum selection of the best alternative to improve the transmission system facilities.

My Section was responsible for the planning of the 345 kV and 138 kV transmission systems interconnecting various designated areas. The Section leader was Charlie, assisted by Bengt and me as Engineering Technician assisting both engineers. These studies were referred to as short-range planning studies. The Load and Energy Forecast Department developed the customer's electrical load and energy consumption forecasts for use in the transmission planning of future facilities of the transmission systems. The studies were referred to as Long-Range Transmission System Planning Studies. We worked daily performing these activities and as time went by, I was becoming proficient at the planning of electric power transmission systems.

The company allowed those that were attending school at night to study during working hours when their work schedule would allow it. I eventually graduated from the NYC Community College in late 1967 with a degree in AAS. As a member of the Transmission System Planning department at AEP, I realized that the AAS degree was below what I needed to succeed further in the electrical engineering world. I also felt that I was smart enough to go further into educating myself. There were other students at the Community College that had plans to go into a four-year degree college. I took note of their plans and comments on the benefits to be derived from further education.

I started thinking about getting an electrical engineering degree. Why not, I thought. I was used to studying at night, had good grades and felt that it made a lot of sense to continue. Then, without any hesitation, very decisive, no misgivings whatsoever in what I was about to undertake despite the many additional years of night schooling, I decided to attend a four-year degree college. I immediately applied for registration at the NYC College in pursuit of a bachelor's degree in Electrical Engineering. I continued working for the AEP's Planning Department.

Charlie or Bengt asked me to perform power flows studies for a given area of the AEP transmission system. I had to use a load flow program to simulate a series of 345 kV transmission system configurations. The results of the computerized studies of the various alternative configurations would be given to them for further analyses. These were part of my daily routine activities. Charlie explained to me that the planning of transmission systems was almost equivalent to the planning of miscellaneous main highways where the objective was to eliminate traffic congestions by adding highway lanes or rerouting traffic to less congested lanes. In the case of electrical systems, the objective was to transfer customer loads that caused transmission lines overload to less loaded lines. Overloads could come from industrial, commercial, and residential consumers as they increased their need for additional electricity delivery due to the expansion of their businesses. Forecasting the load and energy consumption growth of all customers types was the responsibility of a different department. Once a five or ten years annual forecast was developed, it was represented at defined load points during the performance of load flow system studies, allowing us to examine the impact of that growth on the existing carrying capacity of the lines, and therefore, recommendations could be made to replace lines with higher capacity lines or build new lines to reroute the flow of the electrical power to prevent power outages to consumers. The analyses could be performed among counties, cities and among states as needed.

Charlie was studying a specific system configuration to improve the electrical supply to an area suffering from frequent line overloads. As per his request, I simulated a set of specific transmission lines configurations in the computer program used for that purpose. He reviewed the results in detail and then modified or developed alternative means to supply the area under study. I, in my corner desk, simultaneously analyzed the results, developed my own configurations, and selected options to serve the area.

I recalled an instance when I concluded that what was being proposed was not a complete solution to a problem, and that I had found a way to reduce those overloads at a minimum cost (any recommendations made had to be analyzed in detail from an economic viewpoint). I simulated the transmission configuration using the load flow program. I developed a few alternative options, ranked them and brought what I thought was number one to Charlie. Charlie reviewed my recommended option from every angle and concluded that it was the optimum configuration from a technical and economic perspectives. It was the lowest cost alternative, provided enough capacity to alleviate the current overloads and provided reserve capacity for additional growth. The recommended option would cost a few million dollars less and it was feasible to construct. It was the best option out of those that had been studied. He suggested that he would present the recommended alternative to the Department Manager as well as to the upper management for discussion and approval. After additional weeks of further studies such voltage drops, system stability and additional power flow studies, it was concluded that building the many miles of a new 345 kV line would fit perfect with the entire electric system and the line was authorized for construction.

I was obviously very pleased that senior management approved my recommended alternative as presented by Charlie. The line was authorized for engineering, design and construction. Charlie appreciated what I did but never mentioned it to others within the department that it was my idea. It was assumed by everyone that his recommendation was derived from his detailed analyses of the area under evaluation. I could have talked about it to others, but I chose not to because Charlie was a good man, he had trained me and what I knew was the result of his training. He was also a great resource of technical information for me when I needed it. That included answers to school homework although I made every effort not to bother him. I was happy and proud to be working for Charlie and Bengt and for a company with such an elite group of engineers.

A few weeks had gone by when I received a letter regarding the results of my application to NY City College. The Letter indicated that I had been accepted to the NY City College to pursue a degree in Electrical Engineering. I jumped up and down thinking that I would soon begin another phase of my long-range plan to educate myself. There was a stipulation in the letter that I was not too happy with. The Letter stated that out of the 74 credits I had taken at the NYC Community College, the NY City College would accept only 14 credits. I lost 60 credits. However, I was so motivated about becoming an electrical engineer that I did not care.

I thought about it, reviewed City's engineering curriculum, and compared that with the curriculum at the Community College for my Electrical Technology degree and concluded that for obvious reasons I was given only 14 credits toward my engineering degree. The math I had taken at Community College was elementary compared with the advanced mathematics that I would be taking at the four-year college. In a similar manner, the Physics, Chemistry, and Electrical courses were very advanced and therefore not equivalent to what I had taken at the Community College. There were new courses in physics, differential and integral calculus, and many more that I would be taking. There was no problem from my part. I was eager to start school again, almost from inception, and I was better prepared than when I initially started attending the Community College. I was, however, concerned with the math courses. I felt that if I were able to pass a math course on *differential equations,* I would become an engineer. Everyone talked about how difficult that math course was.

My daily routine was to get up early in the morning, get ready to go to the train station, take two trains to reach my office in downtown Manhattan, work at AEP, after a full day of work rush to the train station and to my classes that usually started at 6:00 p.m. in uptown Manhattan, attend my classes and then take three trains back home arriving there about 11:00 p.m. A tough daily schedule over a period of four to five days per week.

I liked my job at AEP. It was new, not boring and I was learning, and whenever I had a better way of performing my work, I told Charlie about it, and if he agreed, the better way was implemented. Charlie asked me occasionally to calculate the voltage drop across the open contacts of a switch. I ran a series of computer studies and determined what the voltage drop would be. I realized that I could get the same results if I used some well-known power system equations. This method saved time by avoiding the use of large computers to make the necessary calculations. The turnaround time from the Computer Center after submitting a deck of data cards was from one day to three days. We had to type the data in a machine equivalent to a giant size typewriter that punched holes in data cards. These data punched cards were placed in the correct sequence on a large deck of cards where each card represented a component of the transmission system. Each card had resistance and reactance values that represented a step-up and/or step-down transformer, a transmission line length and/or a line of distribution system. Generating units were also represented in the same manner.

If you accidentally dropped the deck of cards one could spend days organizing it again to be able to use it to perform computerized studies. This time length was a function of how busy they were with other computer work performed for other departments. Therefore, we had to wait for the computer printouts to return from the Computer Center for analyses. With my simplified method for calculating the steady state recovery voltage across an open switch contacts we avoided the necessity of running various computer runs.

The lengthy procedure was as follows: I had to prepare the number of cases to be analyzed, determine what breaker had to be opened, print the data on specific forms, bring the completed forms along with the deck of cards to the fourth floor where the Computer Center was located, select the cards to be replaced, sit in front of the key-punch machine, transfer the data from the forms to new data cards by key-punching them and then replacing the updated cards individually while taking out the old ones, then submit the deck of cards for computer processing to calculate power flows under a line outage condition. If errors were made while typing the cards, at least two days of delay were experienced. This procedure was lengthy compared to the proposed procedure which reduced the time and cost required to make an equivalent calculation.

Charlie and Bengt reviewed my calculations and agreed with the technical benefits. I wrote a paper which they reviewed, made comments and after the resolution of their comments I brought it to the Transmission Planning Manager who agreed with its submittal to the Transmission and Distribution Magazine (T&D Magazine) for publication. The T&D Magazine, a well-known and prestigious industry publication, agreed to publish it, and it was published on November 1970.

Chapter 24

Electronics Engineering Company

I CONTINUED WORKING FOR AEP while attending evening classes at NY City College. I was following the Engineering Curriculum established by the College. The curriculum included many electrical engineering courses and corresponding electrical engineering laboratories. The laboratories were run by a communications engineer who the students felt was very knowledgeable in the engineering field. A friend, Alberto, a night student and my laboratory partner at NY City College in pursuit of an engineering degree, also worked for AEP. Individually we prepared lab reports for the review of the professor based on experiments performed at the lab.

The professor was very pleased with our performance. One day the Lab professor asked me if I would be interested in working for a company named Decitron, an interesting name in communications, I thought. He was the Chief Engineer of the Engineering Department of Decitron. The company was trying to develop a mobile telephone. I did like the communications field which dealt with small amounts of power in milliwatts rather than in thousands of kilowatts (MW) as in the AEP's electric power systems. I accepted the invitation. I was interviewed and was made a financially attractive offer to work for this communications company. What a mistake that was! I resigned from AEP, a large corporation working for two smart engineers, unselfish and willing to teach me along the way. And I had a very secure job with great benefits. I started working for this company with the hope of getting into a new and challenging field that seemed to have a potential for growth. My friend Alberto was also made an offer an accepted to work for this company.

A few weeks went by and, although the scope of my work was not defined yet, I was getting used to work with miscellaneous, modern, and fancy equipment that I used daily while performing minor work assignments. I noticed that at Decitron Alberto and I were the only employees along with a technical supervisor and the Chief Engineer, our Lab Teacher. Decitron was a small dot in terms of size compared to AEP.

At the end of about seven weeks of working for Decitron, on a Friday afternoon, Alberto and I were confronted with a rather unpleasant surprise. We were being layoff with a commitment that we would be called back to work in a few weeks. We were told that this was a temporary layoff and we should not worry about it.

What to do now? Alberto went back to AEP and applied for his old job. He was fortunate enough to be given back his job. I, on the contrary, did not have enough nerve to show my face in front of my old boss at AEP to tell him "I want my job back". I felt that my pride did not allow me to do that. I had faith that I would get another job; it was a matter of start searching for another one right away.

I updated my resume showing enough detail of the work I performed for AEP and Sterling Corporation and did not include the few weeks I worked for Decitron. Decitron as a communication company was collapsing and I had no desire whatsoever to work in the communications or electronics fields. I mailed my resume to companies that I felt could use the experience I had gained in the electric power systems field combined with the education I had to date (still in progress) and I emphasized my publication in the T & D Magazine during interviews.

It took a couple of weeks until I received a response from Con Edison of New York, the company that provided the electric power supply to NYC and adjacent areas. Con Edison was inviting me to be interviewed by the engineering and system planning departments. I was very pleased that I had a response from a power company. The company was in midtown Manhattan which would be a shorter trip via the subway from my home during my morning ride and in a similar manner a shorter distance to my evening classes at NY City College via a subway ride. I was praying that I would do well during the interviews.

I went to Con Edison motivated to succeed and went through a series of interviews with department managers and engineers of the Generation Planning and the Transmission System Planning departments which were interested in my services. I had no generation planning experience. Consequently, I was not expecting to work for that department.

I received a letter ten days later with an offer to work for Con Edison at their headquarters in midtown Manhattan. Con Edison was and still is one of the nation's largest investor-owned energy companies. Con Edison operated one of the world's largest energy delivery systems which included many miles of underground and overhead transmission power systems. Con Edison provided electricity, gas, and steam to most of NYC and Westchester County.

I accepted the offer and began working for Con Edison as a member of the Transmission Planning Department. I was assigned to assist in the planning of the underground and overhead transmission system. Con Edison imported large amounts of electrical power from generating power plants located in northern New York State and from the generating facilities located across the Canadian border.

I slowly learned a new approach to determine the strengths and weaknesses of NYC existing transmission system facilities. My department was responsible for determining the existing transmission limits to bring the power to load areas under conditions referred to as contingencies. The contingencies could have been the loss of generating units or the loss of one or two transmission lines created by extreme weather conditions or equipment failures. I was excited and proud of my responsibilities and the fact that I was working for a well-known company like Con Edison.

I was still dreaming about traveling the world and working for companies such as AEP and later for Con Edison, two great companies to work for, but there was no hope of traveling anywhere outside their building in the case of AEP. At Con Edison, on rare occasions I went on short trips to the Con Ed facilities located within the NYC and New York State. My dream continued relentless. There had to be a way to satisfy that dream of traveling the world.

While working for Con Edison I continued attending my electrical engineering classes in accordance with my established program of courses. I was getting excellent grades in all my engineering courses. Where I was showing some weaknesses was in a few of the required liberal art courses such as literature, psychology, and writing skills. I was getting above passing grade marks as compared with engineering, physics, and math courses where the lowest grade was a "B".

I was moving along with my schoolwork as fast as I could and as permissible by my available time after work. I attended summer classes to speed up my graduation date. I began searching for better opportunities in the engineering field. My work at Con Edison became a routine type of work and I was expecting to get my engineering degree within one semester or two depending on whether I was able to fit the remaining courses in a semester or wait an additional semester for one or two courses to complete the requirement for a bachelor's degree in Electrical Engineering (BEE).

Chapter 25

Overcoming the Hurdles

I STARTED UPDATING MY RESUME to include my most recent experience at Con Edison. I felt that it was important to have it ready if an opportunity came along. While attending City College at night school, I met another night-adult student who was born in Cuba. We became friends. We had similar objectives for the future and on occasions we studied together. I respected his memory abilities. As an example, we were riding the subway one night on our way home when I told him that I was having a problem with an advanced math problem. He asked me to give him the problem details and I did. He searched his fantastic memory and he started writing the solution while we were riding the train home. I saw him writing and writing on an 8 ½ by 11 inches notebook. When he finished, he ripped two pages full of notes out of his notebook and gave them to me. He derived the complete solution to the math problem. I was amazed! He had the ability to remember math book pages with ease.

Despite his memory ability his intelligence seemed below average when discussing various issues. He had applied for a job at IBM. He was given a series of written tests which he passed effortlessly except for a "common sense" test. He was given several wooden pieces of different shapes to assemble in sequence to form a large figure. He exceeded the time limit and failed the test. He did not get the job.

That led me to believe that although he had the ability to recall visual information such as pages from books, magazines, and license plate numbers in detail after only a brief exposure to it, he lacked the intelligence needed to resolve common sense problems that called for an intelligent approach rather than just memory.

As I found later, good memory is not connected with the person's intelligence level. The popular culture concept of "photographic memory," where someone can briefly look at a page's text and later recite it perfectly from memory is different from seeing vivid images and recalling them in detail later. Photographic memory has never been demonstrated to exist nor has any relation to intelligence. I was pleased that my friend could remember the solution to my problem just by mentally reading the page where a similar problem was found in the math book.

I was almost near graduation as an electrical engineer when I started asking questions about companies that performed work overseas. Ebasco Services, Inc. (Ebasco) was one of those companies. Ebasco engineered, designed, and built power plants to generate electricity, transmission lines to transfer power and distribution lines to distribute electricity to consumers. I said to myself, "that is the company I want to work for." If I could work for a company like Ebasco, I could satisfy my dream of traveling around the world. I realized that I needed additional expertise before I would be sent overseas either alone or as a member of a team.

I found Ebasco's address. They were located at 21 West downtown Manhattan. I mailed them my resume. I was very disappointed that I did not hear from them after a few weeks of waiting. I worked on improving my resume in the hope of making it more attractive to those reviewing it. I mailed it again with the expectation that this time someone from Ebasco would read it. I waited, and waited, and Ebasco did not bother to reply to tell me to forget it.

I did not give up. I had to try again, and if necessary, until someone from Ebasco responded. I felt that if I persisted with determination and a positive attitude, Ebasco would respond eventually. I had nothing to lose and had the time to wait. I mailed my resume for the third time with my usual optimistic attitude. I waited and waited until I said, "that is it!" I had to try another way.

I had heard about employment agencies referred to as "headhunters", that would match individuals that were qualified and experienced to companies searching for individuals with equivalent qualifications. I found one and I went in person to discuss with their representative my qualifications and experience and my desire to work for a company like Ebasco. There were many other companies within and out of NYC that provided engineering, design, and construction services to build power systems anywhere in the world, such as Stone & Webster, Brown & Root, Kaiser Engineering, Black & Veatch, and many others.

I met with the Employment Agent who after reviewing my resume, agreed that I could qualify to work for almost any consulting firm, specifically for my preferred company, Ebasco Services, Inc. I left a few copies of my resume with the expectation that he could help me out since on my own I was not able to. Also, if I could get a job there, the company would pay the agency's fee for their services.

Approximately two weeks went by when I received a phone call from the employment agency indicating that the Consulting Department of Ebasco was interested in interviewing me. I jumped up and down with enthusiasm and of course, pleased that after so many attempts I was finally getting an opportunity for an interview with Ebasco.

I was scheduled to meet a few Senior engineers from the Consulting Department. That department provided consulting services not only to the many engineering departments within Ebasco; civil, structural, chemical, mechanical, soil, foundation, fuels, etc. but also to electric utilities throughout the world. The group of selected individuals was considered by many the engineering elite of Ebasco.

I wore my best suit and tie and went to the interview, allowing enough time for potential train delays to arrive on time. While riding the subway train, I was dreaming and praying that I would be able to pass the anticipated series of important interviews for which the only preparation was my experience working for electric utilities and my night education that culminated in a recent bachelor's degree in electrical engineering. The series of interviews, I thought, could lead to an opportunity of a lifetime.

I started interviewing with the Chief Consulting Engineer, an electrical engineer named George, who asked me many questions and explained the scope of responsibilities of his group and the company. I felt that my personality was also a key factor based on some small talk I had with him. I was also allowed to ask questions about the company. I did not have that many questions and the key question I had was the potential for traveling out of New York city, but I refrained from asking such questions. I emphasized that my primary motive was to work for a company that could make optimum use of my qualifications, experience and ingenuity to improve methodologies to increase efficiency as demonstrated by my engineering article approved for publication by AEP and published in the Transmission & Distribution Magazine. It was only one article, based on common sense, but I felt that I had to show others that I had other abilities. I usually brought with me a few copies of the article for distribution to others upon request. I also brought a copy of the magazine. The idea was to sell myself to those that were interviewing me.

The Chief Consulting Engineer made me realize that I had another asset in my qualifications, my native language, Spanish. A language that I could write, read, and speak fluently. Ebasco provided consulting services to electric utilities throughout South and Central America where Spanish was an asset. George brought me to the office of the next engineer in my schedule of interviews. The subsequent interviews followed a similar form. At the end of each interview, each engineer I met, in addition to asking me many questions, explained to me what they did, and who I would be meeting next.

I was told that I would be interviewed by one of Ebasco's top engineers, a fellow named Frank von Roeschlaub. Frank had worked for Westinghouse, one of the largest corporations in the world that built nuclear power plants and designed motors, generators, turbines, gas turbines and many other related equipment used in the production and transmission of electric energy. Frank had written many engineering articles for the Institute of Electrical and Electronics Engineers referred as the IEEE.

Frank was also the inventor of a special relay to open circuit breakers and interrupt electric power flows timely in transformers and transmission lines protecting miscellaneous equipment. Based on his invention and number of articles he had written; he was selected as the recipient of the 1979 Distinguished Individual Service Award - Power System Relaying. I was privileged and honor to be interviewed by such a well-known engineer in the power engineering industry. I must admit that I was concerned, nervous and tense prior to the interview. I considered that I was not near his engineering level of expertise. I was obviously impressed and had no idea what questions to expect. I wanted to pass all interviews. "Could I understand his questions? Could he come down to my level? Will I be able to answer his questions with some degree of intelligence?" All kinds of concerns wandered through my mind. The sooner I could get to his office the sooner I would get an idea where I stood in the interview process.

The engineer that had just interviewed me brought me to Frank's office who was not there yet, and I was told to wait there. I observed his office while I was waiting for him to return. I thought that for a man of his intellect and popularity within the power industry his office was not fancy, or spacious with an exceptional large desk, and attractive furniture to accommodate clients, or located in a corner of the building and with two windows overlooking the street. On the contrary. The office was rather small, no extra chairs, fancy desk and file cabinets or windows looking toward the outside. It was just a plain and simple office! He was highly revered as a technical member within his Department and the company. It was said that exceedingly technically qualified engineers do not make good managers or preferred not to be in management positions.

Frank returned to his office and I introduced myself. He was tall for my Colombian standards but also, I thought, for USA standards. He was about six feet and four inches. He was skinny and had a very thin mustache. His stature was impressive, inspiring respect. Frank, behind that reputation as a very smart individual, was low key, soft spoken and seemed to be a very nice person. The interview started by Frank asking me questions about my previous assignments which I was able to answer to his satisfaction.

He followed the statements written in my resume specifically related to my experience working for two electric utilities and the company that manufactured power equipment. Frank was fair, no tricky questions. I emphasized that I had been and would continue to be a hard-working person, eager to get the job done. After a few weeks of waiting with eagerness for some sort of communication from Ebasco, I received a letter confirming my appointment to work for the Consulting Department of Ebasco. The salary was significantly higher than what I was making at Con Edison. If my salary had been the same, I would have accepted the offer. I was so delighted to know that after more than a year and half of hurdles, missteps, fails and unsuccessful attempts trying to get a job at Ebasco, I was finally going to be part of the Ebasco family as a member of the Consulting Group.

I thought about continuing studying toward getting a master's degree in engineering once I obtained my electrical degree in engineering, but after discussing it with others, the benefits to be derived from it would not justify my continuing attending night school, I concluded that it was not worth it. I was told that it was better for me to get a Professional Engineer's (PE) license than to get a master's in engineering degree. A PE license was a standard recognized by employers and their clients, governments and by the public as an assurance of dedication, skill and quality. There were many reasons for earning and maintaining a PE license. Only a licensed engineer, for instance, could prepare, sign, seal and submit engineering plans and drawings to a public authority for approval, or to seal engineering work for public and private clients. For consulting engineers, licensure was a necessity. I found that the requirements needed to get a PE license were: 1) of good moral character; 2) at least 21 years of age; 3) and meet education, examination and experience requirements. To satisfy the moral and experience requirements I needed two letters of recommendation from managers and/or engineers that knew me well and could verify my qualifications, experience and moral character. I had no problem getting those two recommendations. The examination consisted of Parts I - Fundamentals of Engineering and Part II – Principles and Practices of Engineering. Each examination was designed to last about a day. One could take each Part at different times or one after the other. I prepared for and took Part I and did not pass it. I was not properly prepared. I went back to study for about two months, until I felt that I was ready and took Parts I and II examinations on two consecutive days and passed both. I was now entitled to have the initials PE after my name as a registered Professional Engineer licensed in the State of NY.

Chapter 26

Gaining Experience

THE CONSULTING GROUP consisted of highly qualified engineers of various disciplines that provided consulting services to electric utilities in the United States and the rest the world. I was apprehensive, concerned, and yet pleased to be part of such an important group. I was worried that I would not be able to fulfill my duties as expected. It was such a huge jump coming from a routine job, a job that once you learned it, became repetitive and boring. I was told during the interviews that my job would not be boring at all. That I could be getting a new assignment weekly, monthly, and that one could have more than one assignment at a time. I could be a member of a team or work individually. Every project was always different, and I had to adapt, do research, and complete projects on time and within assigned budgets. The potential for becoming an asset to the group was there. It was up to me to work hard, learn, be a team member and get the job done. I was told by some of those that interviewed me that I had come across as an engineer that had high potential for becoming a technical asset not only to the Consulting Group but to the company. My inner self was proud yet worried regarding my expected performance. I reported to work on a Monday, at the date and time stated in their letter. I was to report to the Human Resources Department for an orientation session and to fill out some company forms designed for new employees. The morning and part of the afternoon went by very fast. Late afternoon, I was brought to an office that would be my permanent working quarters. I must say that I was impressed with my new office. The desks, although metallic, were of a high-quality material with enough filing cabinets, painted gray and a matching chair with a soft cushion and padded armrests. There was one window facing the outside of the building. The room had a square shape and would accommodate two engineers, I was going to have my own phone and phone number. I was mentally comparing my previous employment at Con Edison where my working desk was located along a row of five desks very close to each other and facing a wooden partition. The wooden partitions ended with a ribbed glass on top the wood. Each of us could hear the man speaking across the partition while he was either on the phone or speaking to his immediate colleague seated next to him. There was no privacy whatsoever. And when you had talkers seated close to you on both sides, it was impossible to get things done.

A new phase toward my life's long-range plan was about to begin. It was a dream in progress that slowly was becoming a reality. As expected, I had to learn the company procedures, get to know my colleagues, and learn the ins and outs of the consulting business. I was captivated by the thought that, depending upon my work performance, one day soon I could take my first trip, perhaps within the

USA to start with, and later out of the country. I felt that after a few months on the job, learning as much as possible from those that were willing to teach me or guide me in the right direction, I was still not ready to undertake a project on my own. I had to be a team member helping others to meet project objectives. I had to earn the right to become a consultant by gaining the necessary expertise, and to keep up with the experts within the consulting group. I was hoping that what seemed impossible at the time, would become easy once I learned it. I was not planning to let others prevent me from meeting my dreams, and this company, through hard work, was the ideal place for me to achieve them. I was eager and motivated to keep my ears and eyes open to get as much technical knowledge as possible. I also needed to improve my writing skills. My Chief Consultant was an experienced project writer and used to review and correct my reports. I had no problem with that since English was my second language, and despite having worked for other good companies, I needed many hours of technical writing to get up to their level. There were specific report formats to follow when writing proposals, interim and final project reports, memoranda, and letters to client addressing client concerns.

Power system consultants had to become proficient at the use of available computer software that was used to perform miscellaneous client tasks. These computer software programs included among others: transmission system load flow, system voltage drops, loss of load probability, distribution system voltage drops and power delivery analysis for industrial, commercial, and residential clients. I learned to use these necessary tools to meet clients' scope of work. I still had a long way to becoming a consultant competent enough for my Chief Consultant to send me on a client assignment. Public speaking was a problem and had to be overcome. When I spoke to a group, I used to get very nervous, hesitant, had a trembling voice and at times I mumbled. This had to improve; public speaking was a necessity and I had to practice many times to overcome what could hold me back in the future.

The Consulting Group had a training system in place which consisted of assigning senior consultants to work with less experienced engineers on new projects. The senior engineer provided the leadership and guidance needed to ensure that the scope of the project would be met in a timely manner, within the allocated budget, and with an acceptable profit margin. That was great. I was constantly learning as the project progressed to completion. I was a quick learner, and on the job-training would put me on the path to success. I appreciated with thanks the learning opportunity.

"It seems impossible until it gets done. Dream big." That was my motto that got me going forward, I made efforts to avoid any steps backwards, unless the circumstances forced me, in which case I had to stop, make corrections, and regain lost terrain to stay on the path to success. I rarely talked with others about my achievements, much less about my failures. I felt that when I spoke to others about my failures, the visual response that I saw or read on their faces was that of satisfaction rather than "I am sorry to hear that."

As time went by, I began to improve my technical and written abilities to get job assignments done as requested, efficiently and timely. No trips yet! No rush! I had to earn them by performing well and convincing my boss I was ready. I would not dare to ask to be sent to some place and then fall flat on my face because I was not fully prepared. I was patient and hoping that I would get there at the right time.

Chapter 27

Domestic Assignments

I WAS PLEASANTLY SURPRISE when I was asked to work on preparing a proposal for a company in San Diego, California. When a proposal was to be written and depending on the type of project, the following steps were necessary: 1) Proposal-Team was organized which included various engineering departments in accordance with the request for proposal (RFP) issued by the client, 2) small projects could require one single department or discipline and a large project could call for the participation of various departments, 3) each department was responsible for a specific section of the Proposal contents in accordance with the scope of work assigned to that department, 4) there was a proposal manager who coordinated the entire Proposal effort, the layout, chapter headings, Table of Contents, Introduction, project description, Executive Summary, proposal's main body, attachments, references, qualifications and experience sections, key staff resumes assigned to the project, and bar charts illustrating project milestones and time lines to completing major tasks, 5) the proposal was reviewed once, twice and as many times as necessary to ensure the presentation quality and the scope of work sections matched the client's RFP, 6) a cost proposal based on the human resources allocated to the project, computer usage, out of pocket expenses such as travel, car rental, hotels, meals, and other miscellaneous charges including an allowance for a reasonable profit margin. 7) the proposal in its final form was submitted to the production department for reproduction of as many copies as necessary, including copies to the library for future reference.

The client received, on an agreed upon date, many proposals from several consulting companies. The client then proceeded to perform a formal evaluation and rank each proposal. The company ranking number one would be selected to perform the project work.

I was gradually becoming an expert on short-and long-range planning of electric power delivery facilities which included generation, transmission, and distribution systems facilities. I was becoming an asset to the consulting group. After about a year and a half, there were no trips scheduled for me yet that my senior management felt confident I could handle.

No problem. I was pleased assisting others as needed and overall with the work I was doing, learning something new every day. At home, the family had grown with the arrival of my son Louis. We managed to purchase a home in the Borough of Queens, NY. Alice and Louis began attending the neighborhood catholic school.

My ability to write proposals, win project awards, manage, and bring projects to successful completion within budget and time schedule had increased. My dream of traveling began to materialize. I was sent on my first trip to San Diego, California, to work on a small project related to studying the performance of a nuclear reactor under certain stress conditions. It may sound like a highly technically complicated project, however, when you work with a competent team, what initially appeared complicated became straight forward analyses. I worked with others in the Computer Department to perform the necessary simulation studies. The work was performed to the satisfaction of the client, General Atomic. The study resulted in a mechanical engineer and I coauthoring an IEEE paper. The paper was submitted for approval to the corresponding IEEE Committee. The Committee approved it and the paper was published by the IEEE Power Engineer Transactions.

My next trip took me to the city of Lakeland, Florida, a city located between the cities of Tampa and Orlando. At the time, the headquarters of Lakeland Electric utility was located on a small piece of property that had one of its property lines abutting a local cemetery. I was assigned an office at the back of the building on the first floor that had a window with a view to the cemetery. My desk was located right in front of that window but facing away from it. Initially, I was always concerned about the scary location of my desk until I got used to the nice and quiet atmosphere. One early and sunny morning I arrived at the office to work, and, as usual, I assumed my regular seating position at my desk facing away from the cemetery. Later that morning I began seeing a strange shadow formed by the sunlight creating what seemed like a human silhouette that was moving his raised arms left and right. This human shadow frightened me. I could not move, I was frozen thinking the worst was happening, that someone buried in the cemetery had gotten out and was calling for help. Every single day of my stay in Lakeland Electric's office had been excessively silent and lonely, then suddenly, while still silent, something was happening. I was afraid! I did not want to turn my head back to see what the cause of those dancing shadows was and began praying that someone would walk into my office and save me. I told myself, during those long minutes of anxiety and heavy breathing, I must look back! I must check the origin of that shadow in front of me moving left and right. I took a deep breath and slowly, very slowly, began turning my head toward the window, and then outside the window, I saw a large body almost glued to the huge window moving his arms left and right having as background the cemetery. I was hysterical, panicked, sweating, and was having short fast breaths, and then, I shouted a savage scream with all my might. When I regained my normal composure, I realized that after observing that figure closely, it was a human being working on the window. He was cleaning the windows. He had rags on both hands and was using them to wipe off the windows with left and right arm movements. Calm returned to me and I began breathing normally and started thinking that this would be an unforgettable event.

Part Three

A Dream Becomes A Reality

Chapter 28

International Assignments

ENIOR MANAGEMENT and specifically my Chief Consultant began to trust my technical abilities. I started traveling alone or with others as a member of an engineering team or as a project team leader managing engineers of various engineering disciplines as a function of project type. I was proud when I was selected to be team leader of a group of qualified engineers. My childhood dream began to materialize when my Chief Consultant said that I would be traveling to Tegucigalpa, Honduras, Central America, to work on a short-term transmission planning project. The project included visits to Managua, Nicaragua, to collect data for the planning of a transmission line that would interconnect Honduras and Nicaragua's electric power systems. My Spanish language became an asset during the performance of work in Spanish speaking countries. I worked in various small engineering projects in Panama, El Salvador, Guatemala, and Costa Rica. I had a significant advantage when compared with other Consulting Engineers that could have been assigned to work in Central American countries due to my fluency in Spanish. This ability allowed me to communicate with my local engineering counterparts; conducting meetings, discussing miscellaneous information both verbally and in writing, all in Spanish.

I was thrilled that I had begun traveling to different countries to perform consulting work and that on my free time, weekends and some nights, and as permitted by my work responsibilities, I would learn about other cultures: customs, food, folkloric dances, traditions, lifestyle, antique buildings' architecture, visiting important sites, some dating back to the Spanish era, and meeting people that spoke with different Spanish accents.

It was also important to bring new client projects to Ebasco and I was fortunate to bring new client work to Ebasco based on my recent project performances and a well-established relationship with satisfied clients. George, my Chief Consultant, told me that I would be traveling to Honduras with him to visit various sites to determine a suitable one to locate a large hydroelectric project. We traveled to Honduras, rented a car with a local driver familiar with the country's roads and started visiting potential sites. There were many dirt and unpaved roads that we had to travel to reach sites that were considered suitable to erect a hydroelectric dam. The scenery was beautiful, the tall green mountains with large fluffy white clouds and a big light blue sky above them created a beyond belief scenery. I was amazed when George selected what seemed the ideal location for a hydroelectric project. Two twin mountains that resembled two tall pyramids, adjacent to each other, were considered ideal by George to locate a hydroelectric power dam that would produce electricity for Honduras with any excess energy generated to be sold to the neighboring Nicaragua. When a dam was built it created an artificial man-made lake behind it. Hydroelectric power was produced as water flowed through the hydroelectric turbines, the dam, and into a river below. The more water passing through the dam the more energy was produced. Ebasco and Motor Columbus, a well-known engineering company at the time, working as a team, were responsible for the engineering and design of the Honduras Hydroelectric Project. I was living the beginning of my dream.

A series of smaller assignments in Central America followed. I returned to Honduras a few more times. I travel to Nicaragua to determine the feasibility of transferring large amounts of electric power via the existing transmission system between Nicaragua and Honduras. I worked on short-term projects in Panama, El Salvador, Costa Rica, and Guatemala. Over a period of a few years I had worked in every country in Central America except Belize, an English-speaking British Commonwealth. Traveling to each of the six countries, starting from the southern border of Mexico to the northern tip of Colombia in South America, I began to appreciate the unique beauty of each country, and the modest living conditions of their people. It was great that I had the opportunity to visit many Central America countries to perform project work.

I never had an assignment in Mexico. However, on my way down to work on projects in Central America I spent time in Mexico, and visited Mexico City, Acapulco,

Bosque of Chapultepec and Chichén Itzá. The latter is considered one of the seven wonders of the world.

Costa Rica, located between the Pacific and the Caribbean, had many attractions such as its beaches, volcanoes, rain-forest jungles, and its great weather conditions with temperatures that range from 70 F to 81 F. This made it the ideal place for Americans to retire.

El Salvador was the smallest and most densely populated Central American country. It exported coffee to other countries, and it had more than 20 volcanoes. I had the opportunity to visit one of its most popular volcanos, the Cerro Verde. It had one of the country's few cloud forests, a great hiking trail, an impressive and frightening view looking down from the edge of a wide volcanic crater semi filled with green sulfuric liquid. The complete round trip to the top and back was about one-day. When we reached the top, my counterpart, an officer from the American Embassy, who spoke Spanish fluently, disappeared out of sight suddenly. I became concerned as to his whereabouts. Where could he have gone? I looked for him, asked questions, and eventually someone told me that he was inside of a nearby hut. I rushed to see him. He had a wet towel over his head and neck to cover all exposed skin completely. "What happen?", I asked. He said, "The bees, yes, the bees." "What about the bees?" I said, "I am allergic to them" he continued, "If I get bitten by one of them, I can get a fatal reaction, and at this altitude, where there are no medical facilities, I will be gone. I have to protect myself." Thank God, all ended well, and we descended from the volcano, and returned to San Salvador safely.

The country at the time was under significant political unrest. I was advised not to leave the Staff House due to the prevailing dangerous situation created by guerrilla activity. Every night around seven o'clock in the evening there were explosions caused by miscellaneous bombs placed at various locations within the city of San Salvador. It was scary, and we had to stay aware of the unsafe conditions. These unsafe conditions existed for many years. At one point, twenty armed guerrillas stormed the Sheraton Hotel in downtown San Salvador and held more than 100 hostages, including several U.S. Green Berets. Releasing of the hostages was negotiated by the government, the Roman Catholic Church, the Salvadorian Red Cross and others. Several days later the violence continued with the killing of a catholic priest and several other Jesuits at the Central American University.

Guatemala, the ancient city of Tikal is one of the largest Mayan sites in Central America and features more than 3,000 temples, pyramids, and other structures. My work did not allow me to visit any important sites, but I was pleased by the opportunity to add one more country to those I had visited already.

I was impressed and identified with Panama because of its original and historic physical connection to Colombia dating back to November 1821 when Panama became part of the Republic of Grand Colombia. The Grand Colombia consisted of Colombia, Venezuela, Panama, and most of Ecuador. Panama is famous for linking Central and South America and the Atlantic and Pacific oceans via the magnificent Panama Canal. The Panama Canal is a famous achievement of human engineering, whose construction began in 1904 under the most severe climate conditions, with uncontrolled diseases such as malaria and yellow fever that were deadly endemic diseases caused by mosquito bites. The crippling effects of these diseases incapacitated many workers and caused at least 20,000 to die, forcing the French to abandon the project, and allowing the United Stated to take over its construction.

The Panama Canal links the Atlantic and Pacific Oceans to create a vital shipping route for large ships navigating from one ocean to the other and avoid traveling to the southern part of South America, around Argentina, and back to the northern areas to cross from the Pacific to the Atlantic oceans and vice-versa. I took a tour of the Panama Canal at the time when ships were crossing the canal. The oceans have different sea levels, and different levels of high tide. At the entrance to the Panama Canal, the Pacific Ocean can rise as much as 20 feet. Ships were raised or lowered at the Canal entrance as a function of the sea levels and the direction they were crossing, the Pacific to the Atlantic or Atlantic to the Pacific Ocean.

Panama also had unrest problems. Many people were protesting for one reason or another the performance of the government. One Saturday afternoon, under beautiful weather conditions, my family and I went out for a walk.

We noticed that people were yelling, jumping and running, and we heard fireworks. My wife suggested "Hurry. Let's go over and participate in the festivities", and we started walking faster toward the large crowds. As we began running, we noticed people were running in the opposite direction. We asked, "Is it all finished?" "No," said someone, "Go back. They are firing real bullets". Then we turned around and started running in the opposite direction, and as we were rushing back, a restaurant owner stopped us and said, "Get in here, quickly", and so we did. And the owner closed the doors. Large crowds were protesting the then President Noriega, a Panama dictator at the time. We had to wait for a few hours until calm was restored, and we could return to our hotel. It is fun, interesting, and a great experience to visit many countries, but it could also be dangerous.

As time passed, other projects developed in various countries in South America. I had project assignments in Caracas, Venezuela, Lima, Perú, Quito, Ecuador and Barranquilla, Colombia, all countries located in the northern part of South América. I worked in Peru not only in the city of Lima, but in the city of La Oroya located at an altitude of 12,287 feet on the Peruvian Andes and about 300 miles from Lima. Traveling to La Oroya by car from Lima, one passes over the Ticlio Mountain located in the Peruvian Andes at an altitude of 14,000 feet. At the top of Ticlio there was a sign in Spanish that read "Necesita Aire?" "Do You Need Air?" At this altitude and La Oroya altitude, visitors arriving from cities located at sea level were affected by the high altitude. Your body must maintain an adequate supply of blood oxygen levels to maintain an acceptable balance of white and red cells. It would take me at least three consecutive days to reach that balance of cells. There were a few times during my trips to La Oroya that I end up at the local hospital in search of a bottle of oxygen.

In Peru I had the opportunity to visit Machu Picchu, one of the best tourist attractions in the world. It is a 15th-century Inca fortress situated on a mountain ridge in the Cuzco Region, Urubamba Providence.

I never travelled further south and would have loved to have visited Argentina and Brazil. I was pleased that my education and the company I was working for, Ebasco, gave me the opportunity to visit the Northern countries of South America, including my native Colombia.

I also performed consulting work in some of the Caribbean Islands such as in the Islands of Jamaica, Dominican Republic, Puerto Rico, Haiti, and Grenada. The islands in general are considered the most beautiful vacation destinations in the world to the point that people have problems in selecting the best island to visit since they are all great but with different attractions

Chapter 29

The World

ASIA, EUROPE, AND AUSTRALIA. I was very pleased with my project assignments in Central and South American countries. While I was working in Peru providing engineering services to Centromin-Peru, a company located in the city of La Oroya, I was the Project Team Leader responsible for all project activities. A member of my team was a very experienced Communications Engineer with specific background in microwave systems. One day we were discussing project activities when he referred to one of his projects in Japan. I got excited and ask him many questions about that part of the world. I was eager to travel one day to Japan and adjacent countries. Time went on until one day my boss told me that Ebasco had just won a project with USAID in the Philippines, and that this project fell within my expertise. I was excited! It would be my first trip to an Asian country. Ebasco at the time had a policy that international travel to some countries would be first class (not sure if as function of distance) for any personnel from the Consulting Department, that included not only flying first class travel but staying at first class rated hotels. I never asked for that, but it was a company policy. Why complain!

There were moments of difficulty and concern. Once you began working on your project at the facilities of the client, one had to be careful on where and what food you ate and what type of water you drank to avoid a grave illness. One evening after eating at one of the best restaurants in Manila, I ordered "Prawns in the Basket" and I got so sick that I had no choice but to see a doctor. The prawns came in a round shaped strainer made from material derived from the sugar cane. I ate contaminated prawns which were supposedly produced on a freshwater pond that was almost dry due to the time of the year. I was away from my project with stomach cramps, diarrhea, and other problems for a period of three days.

I recalled that while traveling to Honduras, the passenger seated at my left gave me "two traveling rules" that I was to follow when traveling to third world countries. He said, "If you cannot peel it, don't eat it", and "Don't drink the water". That is, stay away from lettuces, tomatoes, apples, and other fruits where you might eat the peel. You could end up at the doctor's with food that disagreed with your system, and the same with local water.

I began to enjoy the fruits of my education by not only traveling the world but traveling first class and staying at first-class hotels. My first assignment to Asia was a project in the Philippines working for the Mayor of Olongapo City. Olongapo City was adjacent to Subic Bay, a United States Navy Base. The American Embassy provided me with an Embassy Identification Card that allowed me to get into the Base and use their facilities such as cafeteria, movie theater and other entertainment conveniences. Olongapo, although a nice city, lacked many of the amenities found at the Base. There were many types of entertainment designed for Navy soldiers visiting Olongapo when the Navy ships arrived at the Base.

My office was located at the Mayor's Office and I was assigned a few employees from Olongapo's electric power company to assist me in many of my project activities and analyses. Richard Gordon, the Mayor of Olongapo City, introduced me to various high-ranking government officials of the Philippines such as Mrs. Imelda Marcus, wife of then President Ferdinand Marcus. The Mayor introduced me as "My consultant from South America", although I was an American citizen working for an American company on a project funded by the US Agency for International Development. I completed my project successfully and wrote a corresponding engineering report. It included recommendations to reduce distribution system power losses and recommendations for the best site to locate a substation to supply electric power to Olongapo. I returned to the Ebasco offices in New York after four months in the Philippines.

Ebasco usually identified projects that were within my area of expertise, and where I could be the engineering team leader or, if the project was small enough, I could handle the entire project on my own. The engineering team might have included engineers from other disciplines: civil, soils, communications, protection, and substation design as needed. Next assignments brought me to projects in India, Pakistan, Indonesia, Malaysia, Singapore, and Vietnam.

When I returned to Ebasco, NY from any overseas assignment, after a few days, I was impatient to go back anywhere in the world on another job where I could provide my engineering services. There was a main project in Pakistan funded by USAID. I heard that they were looking for a Chief System Planning engineer. At the time, that was one of the largest overseas projects, close to $100 million US dollars, under the responsibility of Ebasco. The project was of such magnitude that Ebasco had to join forces with two other engineering companies. One was American Electric Power (AEP), a company that I had worked for during the initial phases of my career, and the other one was a smaller company with expertise in revenue collection and billing systems.

I volunteered for the position and after they reviewed my qualifications and expertise based on the many years with Ebasco, I was assigned to Pakistan as Chief of System Planning, responsible for a group of seven consultants. The scope of the overall project was to improve the Water and Power Development Authority (WAPDA) engineering and design procedures, installation and connections specifications and methods, improve field construction and installation of equipment facilities, install computerized software programs, implementation of training programs to ensure adequate revenue collection for electric energy sold to consumers, and prevention of electricity theft by dishonest consumers. The Team was divided into various consulting teams such as Engineering, System Planning, Load and Energy Forecast, Billing, Specifications, Meter Readers, and field supervisors whose responsibility was to make sure that all field work was installed in accordance with specifications. It was a very interesting assignment. Every Consultant was assigned a furnished residential home to make their stay as comfortable as possible. We also had enclosed, gated facilities and two 12-hour shifts guards or gate keepers, referred to as chowkidars.

Every great nation enjoys its own culture. Pakistan's culture was unique due to its Islamic nature and rich historical background. The country's population was 97% Muslims, which was largely divided into two sects, Sunni Islam, and Shias Islam. Shia Islam was practiced by about 15 percent of the Muslims and the remaining of the Muslims practiced Sunni Islam.

There was no English television or radio for home entertainment, nor movie theaters that played American or British movies, nor any movies that had English subtitles. Alcohol was not available anywhere as per a Pakistan decree. There was an American Club that catered to American citizens and to Europeans performing consulting work in Pakistan. The Club facilities included dining, a bar that served alcohol, facilities that played videos during special movie nights, and other entertainment such as organizing teams among the members to play the game of darts. We used to organize round-robin tournaments with teams that consisted of four members from various nationalities: American, Canadian, British, and German and other Europeans professionals working in Pakistan in various projects. Each team was composed of wives and husbands and other family members. We used to play tournaments one night per week for about eight weeks and the winning team would earn a special trophy.

I was authorized to take two two-weeks' vacation period per year, one to go back to the States and another one to neighboring countries not to exceed the distance from Pakistan to Thailand or to England. That is, we could visit any country that fell within a radius formed by those two countries and the company would pay for the airfare.

The Gulf War, code-named Operation Desert Shield for operations leading to the buildup of troops in defense of Saudi Arabia and Operation Desert Storm (January17, 1991 – February 28, 1991) in its combat phase, was a war waged by coalition forces from 35 nations led by the United States against Iraq in response to Iraq's invasion and annexation of Kuwait. Pakistani protesters began to demonstrate on the streets of Lahore against the USA which caused some fears regarding our safety and the safety of our staff in Pakistan. USAID ordered our team to be evacuated to Columbus, Ohio, where we settled for about three months. Upon the issuance of the orders to depart Pakistan, it became difficult to secure airline tickets to travel via Europe to Columbus, Ohio, and the only tickets available were on Air France going east flying over China, Japan, and the Pacific Ocean and eventually arriving in Columbus, Ohio. It was a long flight, about 17 hours, and despite traveling first class it was tiresome. I was pleased that I had completed a trip around the world, initially, traveling over the Atlantic Ocean and Europe to Pakistan, and then traveling over China and the Pacific Ocean back to the States.

After the completion of the Iraqi war, the entire project team returned to Pakistan. I was promoted from Chief System Planning to General Manager of the Ebasco Company facilities in Pakistan. I was responsible for all WAPDA project activities, including all department chiefs and foreign consultants, and Pakistani field subcontractors. The team, Ebasco and AEP, with Ebasco as the lead consultant had about 900 employees with the majority being Pakistani field personnel.

Chapter 30

Independent Consultant

THE PAKISTANI PROJECT was near completion and all-American staff had to return to the States or to Europe back to their respective home offices. The company knew in advance that the project soon would come to a successful completion, and that they must be ready with a new assignment not only for me but for others returning home to NY. The company was having problems getting new domestic or overseas project work and saw the need to downsize personnel. The approach used to downsize the company staff was to layoff personnel based on their salaries. Highly paid consultants would be laid off first if they were without project assignment, followed by the next lower paid engineer. Those with high salaries were considered an expense of the company's overhead regardless of the employee's expertise, past performance and benefit to the company. Upon my return to NY, Ebasco had no project assignment for me and therefore, regardless of my qualifications and experience, I was laid off. I left Ebasco Services two months later after my return from completing successfully my assignment as the General Manager and closing the project in Pakistan, and after working for Ebasco Services for over 21 years. The Pakistani project was completed on schedule and within the assigned budget.

I was concerned for a few days, until I decided to establish a one-man consulting firm and started mailing my resume to the companies I was familiar with. I began working for a company out of Washington, DC that sent me on a gas turbine project assignment to Barranquilla, Colombia. After Colombia, and as an independent consultant, I was hired by Resource Management International (RMI), a Californian consulting company to work on a project funded by the US Agency for International Development based in the Philippines. Later I worked for another consulting company from the State of Vermont on a project in Malaysia. A Consulting Company located in Washington DC subsequently hired my services for a project in Nigeria, an African country on the Gulf of Guinea. Nigeria's capital city Abuja had over 250 ethnic groups, and several religions that included Muslim 50%, Christian 40%, and indigenous beliefs 10%. The country speaks over 500 languages. English was designated as the country's official language to facilitate the cultural and linguistic unity of the country's post-colonization by the British.

We arrived at the capital, Abuja, and stayed at the Sheraton Abuja Hotel. We were given special instructions regarding our personal safety while in Nigeria. It was recommended that all payments be made in cash. It was not safe to use credit cards anywhere, including the hotel, supermarkets, restaurants, and other local businesses due to the potential for fraudulent charges latter appearing on our credit card. To resolve the problem, there was a man from the Nigerian electric utility assigned to carry a small bag full of Nigerian Naira, the Nigerian currency. He was responsible for paying hotel charges, meals, car rentals, and other miscellaneous incidentals related to the project. We had to travel via car rental to the rural areas located Southwest of Abuja not too far from Lagos, the largest Nigerian city. I was carrying a small bag with a zippered pocket and a shoulder strap that I never let go and used to carry miscellaneous project documents, and some clothes to change as needed. I also had a green sports jacket that I took with me for special meetings, and I had the habit of placing my passport in the inside pocket of my jacket. When we were traveling in the car rental, I placed my jacket in the trunk of the car. Big mistake! We arrived at our destination and I checked in our hotel. Then I realized that my jacket was still in the car, I rushed outside to ask the driver to open the trunk, but he was gone. This car rental was not part of a well-known car rental company, it was a driver that was outside the hotel waiting to be hired. What to do? I shared my worry with my teammates, and no one had an answer or seemed very concerned about it.

The many recommendations made about personnel behavior, and here I was, an experienced traveler, making a serious mistake in a country that at the time was well known for corruption in almost every aspect of life you can think of. What to do? I went back to the hotel room worried that I would not be able to get out of Nigeria as scheduled. I arrived at my room, laid down on my bed, and started thinking that I had committed a serious blunder. My thoughts were directed toward the following day calling the American Embassy to report the loss of my Passport. I gazed around my room, saw my carryon bag on a chair and thought about getting ready for the next day's project work. I unzipped the top center main pocket and took out some of my documents for review. I needed a pen, unzipped another smaller bag pocket to get a pen out. Surprise! Surprise! A pleasant surprise. I had placed my USA Passport in the outside pocket of my carryon bag, something I rarely did. Problem solved! The next day I did not mention it to anybody, and nobody bothered to ask me if I had found it.

I was fortunate that after I left Ebasco, I always found various consulting firms that could use my services on overseas project assignments. Project work kept coming my way at a satisfactory per diem rate.

Chapter 31

Serious Accident

I WAS HIRED by International Resources Group (IRG), a company out of Washington DC, for a project located in the State of Haryana, India, a project funded by USAID. The Team responsibility was to identify the causes of a low degree of transmission system reliability such as frequent transmission line outages causing loss of power to areas of the Haryana system. I had to visit the various system facilities and conduct interviews of system operating personnel. I used to travel along the Northwest Haryana to the Southern Haryana to meet project objectives.

As the Team Leader with a few consultants, we recommended to our client the purchase of new modern equipment designed to measure the electrical distribution system power losses. The team was working at the Pinjore Substation, in Panchacula, the city where our engineering team was staying at a local hotel. The utility assigned a lineman to work on opening a 4kV power line with complete disregard for safety. I was not present when the lineman was setting up the available metering equipment to take readings. The equipment used was not designed to perform this type of readings and much less the lineman's setup.

I was called to inspect the setup and what I saw was unacceptable and very dangerous. There were a few men around the testing setup, and I immediately told everyone to back away from it. There was one man too close and I raised my arm to protect him. I protected him, but unfortunately a 4kV electric spark occurred, and I had electricity flowing down the right side of my body. I collapsed to the ground unconscious. I was taken to the local hospital by an ambulance and as they were carrying me in a stretcher toward the inside of the hospital, I woke up for a few seconds and said, "I am not going to die yet! I have two small children to take care of," and I passed out again.

The date of the accident was September 29, 1998. The American Embassy in India responded effectively and promptly and started a search for the best hospital to take care of my second-degree burns, over 40% of my body was burned as indicated by a local doctor. The comments made by others were that the expectations for survival were low but possible. I was told that hospitals in three cities were considered, London, England, Bangkok, Thailand, and Haifa, Israel. It was decided that the best hospital for my severe conditions would be the Herzliya Medical Center located in the City of Haifa based on their many years of experience dealing with patients with burns derived from the conflicts between Israel and neighboring countries.

The Herzliya Medical Center assigned Doctor Yitech Ramon and a nurse, to fly to New Delhi from Haifa on a dedicated airplane to pick me up and fly me back to Israel.

I was unconscious for a few days including during the transportation by ambulance from the hospital in New Delhi to the Indira Gandhi International airport.

When the stretcher was lowered from the ambulance and brought over to the airplane gate, Doctor Ramon woke me up and asked me, "Can you get out of the stretcher and load the plane?' I said, "Yes, I think I can" and so I did. I did hear Doctor Ramon saying, "I believe he is going to make it!" I don't remember that I was in any pain, perhaps because I was under the effects of a drug for the pain. I was at the Herzliya Medical Center for about seven weeks until I was told I could travel back to my home in the USA. I was still recuperating but I could travel. I was left with many burn scars on the entire right side of my body but alive. Traveling to and from Israel under those conditions was certainly not in my world travel plan. I was brought back to the States accompanied by a nurse assigned by the Herzliya Medical Center in Haifa to ensure my wellbeing during the long flight. My recovery period lasted for an additional three months.

Chapter 32

Wonders of the World

I VISITED SIX out of the seven world continents, Antarctica was the exception. In some countries, I visited as many as six or more cities depending on the scope of work of my project. In the Philippines, my engineering team consisted of six consultants and support staff, a secretary and a driver. (See photograph at the bottom of Page 221). We traveled by van or by boat to many cities and islands to examine each electrical distribution system and to develop recommendations to improve their operating efficiency. In many other countries we assembled similar teams and traveled to many locations as called for by the project's scope of work.

When I was assigned to projects that were in Asia or Africa, I had to travel via Europe on my way to these assignments, and I usually took a few hard-earned vacation days to visit European countries or when in location, I visited neighboring countries. In a similar manner, if my assignment was in Australia, I would travel via the West Coast, and over the Pacific Ocean, and make two or three-day stopovers in San Francisco, Hawaii, or New Zealand, either on my way to Australia or on my way back to New York City.

BORN TO TRAVEL THE WORLD

I was blessed with the opportunity to visit five of the seven wonders of the world along with two of my children. The five wonders of the world that we visited at different time periods over my career included: 1) The Great Wall of China- Beijing, China, 2) Machu Picchu-Peru, 3) Roman Colosseum-Rome, Italy, 4) Taj Mahal-Agra, India, 5) Chichen Itza, México. I did not have the opportunity to visit the remaining two wonders of the world; 6) Petra-Jordan and 7) Christ the Redeemer Statue-Brazil. What follows (See photographs Pages 220 - 223) are various photos selected from my family album of the five Wonders of the World that my children and I visited at different times over my career. Appendix B, Tables 1 and 2, lists other countries and treasures of the world I visited at different times throughout my career. A brief description follows:

1. The Great Wall of China - Beijing, China. We visited the Great Wall of China while on an assignment in Pakistan. It was a short flight from Lahore, Pakistan to Beijing, China. The wall was built more than 2,000 years ago to keep invaders from crossing its northern border. We climbed the wall as high as we could under beautiful weather conditions. We were impressed with what the Chinese people were able to build under the conditions prevailing at the time. In the photo shown on Page 222, my son David is on the top of the China Wall waving back at me while I was taking the photograph.

2. Machu Picchu - Peru, was another tourist attraction that we were able to visit during my many project trips to Peru. Machu Picchu has been considered another wonder of the world. It was built during the ancient Inca civilization of Peru. It is in a remote location in the Andes and referred to as the lost city of the Incas with its complex and intricate stone buildings. The peak at its highest point has an altitude of 8,835-foot. It was discovered in 1911 by Hiram Bingham III, an American explorer, and it has been a source of fascination throughout the world ever since. You must travel via a scenic train from Cusco to get to Machu Picchu.

3. Roman Colosseum - Rome, Italy. Rome is the Eternal City, home to many ancient treasures. The Colosseum, however, is a treasure worthy of being referred to as a wonder of the world. This massive arena, where gladiators fought to the death, was built around 80 A.D., and it held 50,000 people seated in row levels placed one above the other. Climbing to the top levels not only gives great views of the limestone structure but also over Rome itself. This visit combined with the attractions of Rome was unforgettable. I took a few vacation days while I was on my way to my project in Pakistan. It happened that during my stop in Rome, I, along with many tourists, visited the Sistine Chapel, which is within the Apostolic Palace, the official

residence of the Pope, in Vatican City. While admiring Michelangelo's paintings, I met an Ebasco senior Vice President, my boss reported to him. I was concerned about this unexpected encounter, but there was no problem, I was meeting project objectives, and in addition he was also sightseeing. We were thousands of miles away from the main office and we both were sightseeing at Sistine Chapel. Amazing! We spoke for a while and I explained that I was on my way to Pakistan and had taken a few days off.

4. Taj Mahal - India, was another of my favorite visits to the ancient world. I had the opportunity to travel to the Taj Mahal on the southern bank of the Yamuna River in Agra. It is a monument to love. It was built in the 17th century by Mughal emperor Shah Jahan to house his beloved late wife Mumtaz Mahal. It is built with white marble, with an arched central tomb and surrounding minarets. It is one of the world's most recognizable and beautiful buildings, especially at sunrise and sunset. (See photo of my daughter Marie and my son David and myself in front of the Taj Mahal, Page 221). On another occasion while assigned to Pakistan on a similar project, I came back with my son Louis and his wife Laura. It is a worthwhile place to visit.

5. Chichén Itzá - Mexico. It is a complex of Mayan ruins on Mexico's Yucatan Peninsula. A massive steep a 78-

foot, pyramid-shaped temple, known as El Castillo, dominates the ancient city which thrived from 600 A.D. to the 1200s. It is known for its Mayan sites, including Tulum, above the Caribbean Sea, with its nine-tier pyramid. At the time, we did climb the steps to the top of the pyramid, but today you can no longer reach the top by foot.

BORN TO TRAVEL THE WORLD

World Photographs Family Album

My children Marie and David in The Egyptian Pyramids, Africa.

The Great Sphinx of Giza   The Pyramids, Egypt

The Lahore Mosque, Pakistan   The Giant Buddha, Japan

LOUIS RODRIGUEZ

World Photographs Family Album (Cont.)

Visited five of the seven wonders of world and traveled around the world twice. The photographs are courtesy of my family album.

The Alhambra, Grenada, Spain   The Sacred Family Cathedral, Barcelona, Spain

The Sacred Family Cathedral, Barcelona, Spain   Bangkok, Thailand

World Photographs Family Album (Cont.)

Amsterdam, The Netherlands

The Parthenon, Greece

The Taj Mahal, Agra, India

Jumbo Kingdom, Floating Restaurant, Hong Kong

MacArthur Return to the Philippines
Monument. My Engineering Team

Engineers in Training

World Photographs Family Album
(Cont.)

My son David waving at me. China Wall, Beijing, China

Tiananmen Square, Beijing, China

Barcelona Cathedral, Spain

My daughter Marie and my son David at the China Wall, Beijing, China.

Chapter 33

Dream Made a Reality

IN LOOKING BACK to my humble beginnings to the fulfilment of a long range objective, my journey included: attending second and third grades elementary schooled, learning a trade as per my mom's guidance, going through child-labor exploitation to eventually becoming a silversmith, traveling to the USA, serving in the USA armed forces, getting a GED, working during the day and studying at night, and eventually earning a bachelor's degree in electrical engineering which opened many doors that allowed me to reach my dream of traveling the world.

My attitude was always positive. It was not always easy to complete the various phases needed toward a better future. There were many hurdles, missteps and falls and hard work was needed to overcome these obstructions in my path to success.

On my way to meet planed objectives, I found coworkers and sometimes friends that were willing to help without expecting a reward in return. I also found those individuals that were not dependable, that pretended to be friends, that spread hurtful gossip and that did not hesitate to open your desk for their benefit while you were away. I had to stay alert to protect myself from these individuals. As an example, upon my return from one of my project trips, my written work-in-progress related to a new idea for another project was removed from my desk without my authorization. An individual took my draft document and finalized it. He published the engineering article under his name, bragging about it to others on how great his work and his personal efforts were that his article had been published in an industry magazine. It did not happen often, but it happened, and usually when I was away from my office.

I had a passion for physical exercise, perhaps as a means of entertainment and to keep myself in good physical condition while I was away from home. I used to play squash, racquetball or tennis when I was on an assignment.

I was proud of dreaming big, that I was always motivated, completed my college education at night, and became a well-known consultant throughout the power engineering industry. I always had a positive attitude and a competitive enthusiasm to win, excellent work ethics, worked late and on weekends as needed to get high quality work completed, and do things that were outsize my comfort zone.

Others wanted to become businesses owners, lawyers, and chefs, to live an extravagant and luxurious life without getting out of their immediate surroundings. At times, it seemed impossible to meet planned goals until goals were achieved. I strode confidently up the ladder of personal achievement and today I can claim that "I was born to travel the world" and that, "I am happy. I did it!".

I have a family that includes two lovely daughters, Alice, and Marie, and two sons, Louis, and David. My daughter Alice is happily married to Jim a mechanical engineer and a successful business owner. They have three children, two boys and one daughter.

Pictured, starting at left end are grandson Callum, daughter Marie, granddaughter Kata, son in-law Dane, son in-law Jim, daughter Alice, Lylia, Roxy, grandpa Louis, son David, daughter in-law Kyomin, grandson Scott, granddaughter Alexa, and grandson Stephen. Courtesy of photographer German Valencia.

The two boys, Stephen and Scott, are already pursuing careers in engineering, Alexa, upon graduation from high school, plans a career in medicine or some related field. My daughter Marie is also happily married to Dane and they have two children, Callum and Kataryna. Marie and Dane are college graduates. They both work for the US government in Washington, DC. The extent of their responsibilities takes them all over the world. I always felt that Marie followed in my footsteps in traveling the world. My son Louis, married to Laura, (not shown on the photograph) also both college graduates, and making optimum use of their education. Louis owns his own firm that provides consulting services to capital venture companies. My son David, the youngest, is a successful consultant, married to Kyomin, both with college degrees. David offers legal solutions and automation services to plaintiff law firms.

My children went away many years ago to form their respective family lives. I dearly love all my children and I appreciate the need for their independence. They live far away from me and from each other with their respective families. My two daughters visit me with some frequency and especially when significant health issues have affected me. Louis left home after completing college. He worked for large corporations and eventually set up his own consulting firm. However, he distanced himself from his family. He abandoned us after graduation from college. His family dislike, perhaps, was caused by my absence during his youth at critical times. However, I love and admire him for having a successful career and a good relationship with his wife and daughter Nicole. And then there is Roxy who has been my *life extension* companion for over 20 years. She has provided me with care-given assistance at critical moments of my life. Roxy has been there at those moments when one experiences the negative effects of loneliness and miscellaneous health issues.

I was able to realize my childhood dream of traveling the world and I have achieved almost anything that I was motivated and promised myself I would do. I always believed that if you commit yourself to get it done, you will get it done despite the many roadblocks found on the path to meeting objectives. I considered myself selfish because I have always been concerned with my own interests, do whatever it takes to get to the finish line before the other guy and without hurting anyone. I believe that despite what many may think of being selfish, it is an attribute that enabled me to fulfill my dream of the world.

Over the years, traveling had a serious impact on my family life. My desire for traveling was so strong that I neglected my wife and children, although I never stopped loving them. To my regret, when I look back, I think that I could have been a better husband and father. In my career there were many successes and a few failures due to my determination for traveling. I considered myself a person with good feelings but one that was absent from my family duties many times due to the pursuit of my personal dream.

After 23 years of living out of a suitcase, I felt that it was time for me to settle in one place. Upon my return from one my trips, my Ebasco Services boss, Cono Petrizzo, suggested that prior to the completion of the Pakistani project, I should buy a place that I could call home and recommended that I buy a home in New Jersey. And so, I did.

After settling in NJ, and having stopped traveling overseas, I felt the need to stay busy. One day, I was listening to the radio when I heard that a well-known company, Morgan Stanley, was looking for Financial Advisors. I applied. I was interviewed and I was offered a low but acceptable salary, and I accepted. I was trained for a two-year period to become a financial advisor. After the completion of the training course, I had to take written examinations to obtain a series of licenses that included the Series 7 license, the most difficult to get, along with others such as Series 63, 65 and 31, all necessary to becoming a financial advisor. I became a qualified Financial Advisor and worked in that capacity for Morgan Stanley, Merrill Lynch and Met Life.

After retiring as a financial advisor, I was chosen by a

group of business owners to serve on a volunteer basis, as the Executive Director of the Latino Chamber of Commerce of Monmouth County, New Jersey, from 2005-2013. The Chamber initiated activities with

Lt. Governor Kim Guadagno, Leo Cervantes owner of La Playa restaurant and Louis Rodriguez, Executive Director Latino Chamber of Commerce, along with members of the business community that gathered for the ribbon-cutting ceremony of the official opening of the La Playa restaurant. Courtesy of photographer German Valencia.

12 members that were dedicated to serving the Latino business owners. The Chamber organized many seminars and networking events for business owners, and ultimately, the Chamber grew to 250 members. It is important to

establish meaningful relationships with key members of the community for the benefit of the business community and those in need. The former New Jersey Lt. Governor, Kim Guadagno, was a strong supporter of the Latino Chamber and together we worked for the benefit not only of Monmouth County but for the entire State of New Jersey. We worked together assisting Latino business owners at critical moments when they needed financial solutions to distressed conditions affecting their businesses. I continue supporting the community enthusiastically through many activities. Among others, I was nominated to the Board of Trustees of the Educational Facilities Authority (EFA) by the then New Jersey Governor Chris Christie and Lt. Governor Kim Guadagno, confirmed by the NJ Assembly and Senate for appointment.

I am currently serving as a Trustee of the Parker Family Health Center Board of Directors; an organization close to my heart whose mission is to provide free health care to members of the community who cannot afford health insurance. I am also serving as Trustee on the Board of Directors of Monmouth Medical Center- Jainabad Health, the Community YMCA, and the Wilbur Ray Scholarship Committee at Brookdale Community College, important nonprofit organizations.

David Prown is a business owner with a good heart, who in his spare time provides tutorial services to young Latino students attending the Brookdale Community College at night in search of a better future. David and I cooperate with each other assisting students in financial need. David identifies those students and I, as a member of the Wilbur Ray Scholarship Committee at Brookdale Community College, assist nominated students in complying with the requirements for a scholarship. The Scholarship Committee reviews the students' applications and approves or rejects them as appropriate. Those students that are qualified obtain a scholarship to support their education with the award based on academic and other achievements.

It is certainly a good feeling to look back at your humble beginnings, your hurdles, falls and accomplishments, and appreciate what one has done through hard work, resilience, discipline, enthusiasm, and positive attitude and that your dreams were made a reality. I also acknowledge with thanks the many opportunities that I was given by this great country, the United States, which allowed me to turn ambition into achievement and for which I am pleased to continue giving back through my community services, working as a volunteer in various organizations to make a difference. (See Appendix A).

The writing of this book was another dream that I was eager to bring to conclusion. Getting to the last chapter was not an easy task but I got it done. It is my hope that these writings inspire many readers to dream big and to achieve what seems unachievable. It must be understood that dreams don't become a reality through magic. It takes a positive attitude, determination, hard work and sweat.

Chapter 34

What Happened to My Childhood Friends?

I returned to Colombia a few times after many years of being away from my mom and friends. I went back for the first time after graduating from college with an electrical engineering degree. That was thirteen years after departing Colombia in 1962. I went back again in 1975 along with my wife Lylia and our two children, Alice and Louis. I was told by a neighbor that my mother had suffered immensely from my departure for many years. I wrote her letters over that time period but not with the frequency that she deserved. I served in the army and then I concentrated on educating myself for a better tomorrow. After 13 years I was already working as an engineer. It was not a good excuse, and I could not explain to anyone why I didn't write often. I just never did. I neglected my brother, maybe due to my personal ambition and desire to get to my destination fast.

I returned to see my family when I felt that I had something to justify my absence and for which they could be proud. My brother Adolfo and uncle Bernardo came to pick us up at the airport. My brother was a grown-up man, exhibiting a mustache and sideburns and speaking Spanish using slang words that I was not used to hearing. My mom and uncle were older, as expected, but they had not changed significantly as compared to my little brother Adolfo who was not little anymore. Two days went by talking to my mother about my life in the USA, my adventures, successes and failures, until the third day when suddenly I became emotional, perhaps reacting to the fact that I had not seen my mom for many years. I started crying like a little baby. I had a hidden emotion of many years. I burst out into tears and could not stop crying, and those around me, my mom, wife and children could not find a way to console me. After a long while I stopped the shedding of tears and I asked my mom about my friends: Rafael, Horacio and Marco. All had gone away in the pursuit of their careers. Rafael had become an architect, married and was living in Barranquilla, Colombia. Horacio was an officer in the military, and nobody knew his whereabouts and Marco married a wealthy lady from an upper-class Colombian family and had left Colombia for the United States.

I began traveling all over the world and never heard from my friends again until many years later when I stopped traveling and went back to Colombia again to visit my family. I stopped to visit Juan, the younger brother of Rafael and Pedro, at the jewelry store in downtown Bogota. The store was still there, no change whatsoever. We spoke for a while about the old days although Juan was not a close friend that we used to hang around with. He gave me an update regarding his brothers and other mutual friends. Rafael was living in Bogota again. Marco, by coincidence was visiting Colombia at the time of my visit, and Horacio was nowhere to be seen. I obtained contact phone numbers and we agreed to meet for lunch with Rafael, Pedro and Marco. We met for lunch and shared stories from the old days. I found out that Marco was living with his wife in New Jersey not too far away from where I was residing, a pleasant surprise. Rafael was still working as an architect, but I could sense that he was not working as a successful one. He had divorced his beautiful wife whom I had met earlier in one of my trips to Colombia. He was living with a lady that had an adult son and all shared a rented apartment. It seemed to me that he was under the control of this lady based on one of a few phone calls that I made to his place, and while we were talking, I heard a woman's voice screaming in the background, "Who are you talking to, get off the phone." He explained, "I am speaking to United States, please." I felt sorry for Rafael based on what I heard during the phone call, someone in the background manipulating and bullying him. I felt that he was living under horrific conditions that seemed to be deteriorating by the minute due to the lady he was living with, in addition to poverty.

Marco, although did not finish college, was living a better life in West New York, New Jersey, in a condominium apartment owned by his wife who seemly derived a monthly income from her Colombian family. He got along very well with his wife. The problem he had was that he became a heavy wine drinker. I invited both to my place, in Central Jersey, and both came once during the summer season and stayed for two days. My swimming pool was open, charcoal was burning, the hamburgers, hot dogs and corn were being grilled and ready to be served. They had a good time. He was impressed with my large home, and the sleeping quarters I provided, and I conveyed that I was not by any stretch of the imagination wealthy, I was just financially healthy, I had earned a decent living throughout my professional hard-working life.

I had expected that my early childhood friends, because of their early beginnings, attending expensive private high schools and colleges, with strong support from their wealthy families, would have reached top levels in the military, in the industry or as entrepreneurs in various enterprises, and would be the envy of many with their success. However, that was not the case. They had had short-term rises in their careers which they were not able of sustaining on a permanent basis.

Pedro, I believe, never finished college but became a successful buyer and seller of precious stones; emeralds, diamonds and other stones. He rose to be a wealthy trader following in the footsteps of his father, Don Pedro. However, certain dealings with unscrupulous individuals forced him to transfer his assets to his wife to protect them from debtors as was explained by Marco. This was the reason for the collapsing of his wealth. His ex-wife refused to return his assets and later she ran away with Pedro's lawyer. Again, a short-lived success. Juan on the other hand, inherited the jewelry store from Don Pedro, and was able to run it successfully and made a decent livelihood out of it for him and his family.

I found out that Horacio was not an officer in the military any longer, that he worked for an insurance company, Colpatria, a well-known Colombian company, where he rose to the position of International Business Vice President responsible for Central and South American countries bringing new business to Colpatria. In later years, although not clear why he left such a successful career, he associated himself with a trusted friend to set up a car dealership. It appears that his dear friend after some time cleaned out the business bank account and other company assets resulting in the bankruptcy of the dealership business. Horacio ended up owing large amounts of money to supposedly "mafia" connected individuals who had provided funds on a loan basis for Horacio to get the dealership business back up into a successful operation. After the cash injection, the dealership failed, and Horacio was unable to pay back the loan. The bad fellows threatened to break his knees, one at the time, until the full amount was paid. He feared for his life and ran away to Miami. In Miami, he was not able to get a high paying job as a professional business person, perhaps his English ability was weak combined with the lack of experience working for American companies, and he ended up working as a guard for a company that provided protection services to commercial and industrial businesses.

When I listened to Marco, Rafael and Pedro describe their achievements and failures over their entire lives, as well as to Horacio's, story, I compared them to my life, and what I was able to achieve through motivation, persistence and believing that if one makes the effort one can reach the pinnacle of success that initially appeared difficult to climb, but once you are at the top, you may say, "That was not too bad after all". The whole idea of writing this book was to share with the readers that you don't get into something to test the waters but to make waves.

Appendix A

Summary of Accomplishments

Main Accomplishments

I have provided consulting services to electrical utilities throughout the world working on projects funded by the United States Agency for International Development (USAID), The World Bank, the International Development Bank (IDB), US Trade Organization and others. I held positions of Vice President, General Manager, Executive Director, Manager, and Chief of Party successfully.

Publications – Community Services - Achievements and Awards

Publications. I have written technical papers published in the following industry and/or trade magazines: Institute of Electrical Engineers (IEEE) Power Apparatus and Systems Transactions, The Electrical World, Transmission & Distribution-USA., Transmission & Distribution-International. I coauthored The Electric Distribution Power Systems Manual developed by Ebasco Services Inc and Published by McGraw-Hill Publishers for use by electric utilities throughout the world.

Community Services. I have provided and continue to provide services to the community on a volunteer basis, at the time of this writing I was a Trustee in the following Boards;

1. New Jersey Educational Facilities Authority (EFA), nominated by former Governor Chris Christie, and approved by the New Jersey Senate.

2. The Red Bank YMCA.

3. Monmouth Medical Center, RWJ Barnabas Health.

4. The Parker Family Health Center.

5. Member Wilbur Ray Scholarship Committee at Brookdale Community College.

6. Former Trustee of the Boys Scouts of America Monmouth County Council, Family and Children Services, Long Branch and Monmouth County Art Council.

Achievement Awards. Received numerous awards and recognitions from various organizations among others the following:

LOUIS RODRIGUEZ

1. Boys Scouts of America, Northeast Region, Scoutreach Conference, keynote speaker, Eagle Scouts Medal, 2017.
2. NJ Educational Authority (EFA) Certificate of Appreciation as a public board member, 2017.
3. Monmouth Medical Center special award in the form of a Cristal Table Clock issued for a job well done as a Trustee in the Board of Directors.
4. George Perrot McCulloch Award for Leadership, Kean University, November 2013.
5. Red Bank Regional High School the Source Outstanding Community Partnership Award, 2011.
6. Monmouth County Prosecutor's Office Certificate of Appreciation, October 2010.
7. Latino American Association of Monmouth County Award for Outstanding Contribution, Dedication and Community Service, October 2006.
8. Certificate of Special Congressional Recognition, Congressman Frank Pallone, October 2006.
9. Tu Sello Latino Market Award for Contributions and dedication to the Community, September 2006.
10. Brookdale Community College Leadership Shore Certificate of Recognition, 2004.
11. Morgan Stanley Dean Witter Certificate of Achievement Financial Advisor, July 2000.

Appendix B

Table 1-Partial List of Countries Visited

TABLE 1
VISITED SIX CONTINENTS - FIFTY FIVE COUNTRIES AND MANY CITIES

Africa	Australia	Asia	Asia (Cont.)	Europe	North America	North America (Cont.)	South America
Cote d'Ivoire	Australia	China	Saudi Arabia	Denmark	Barbados	Honduras	Colombia
Egypt		India	Singapore	France	Canada	Jamaica	Ecuador
Nigeria		Indonesia	South Korea	Germany	Costa Rica	Mexico	Peru
		Israel	Sri Lanka	Greece	Dominican Republic	Nicaragua	Venezuela
		Japan	Taiwan	Italy	El Salvador	Panama	
		Malaysia	Thailand	Netherlands	Grenada	Trinidad & Tobago	
		Maldives	Turkey	Norway	Guatemala	USA	
		Pakistan	United Arab Emirates	Spain	Haiti	Puerto Rico	
		Philippines	Vietnam	Sweden			

Table 2-Other World Treasures Visited.

- Opera House, Sídney, Australia
- Niagara Falls, New York, USA
- Tallest Building in the world, Dubai, UAE
- Leaning Tower of Pisa, Rome, Italy
- Tiananmen Square, Beijing, China
- Mount Fuji, Honshu Island, Japan
- Victoria Peak, Honk Kong
- Reclining Buddha, Bangkok, Thailand.
- Eiffel Tower Paris, France

Made in the USA
Coppell, TX
17 June 2022